4-6-73

GOLD RUSH NARROW GAUGE

The Spell of the Yukon

•

"The winter! the brightness that blinds you..."

GOLD RUSH
NARROW GAUGE

·

~ by CY MARTIN ~

The Story of the White Pass and Yukon Route

 TRANS-ANGLO BOOKS

Los Angeles, California 90053

·

SPENCER CRUMP
Editorial Director

GOLD RUSH NARROW GAUGE

The Story of the White Pass and Yukon Route

FIRST EDITION

Book Design: Hank Johnston

Library of Congress Catalog Card No.: 71-96823

SBN 87046-001-3

Printed and Bound in the United States of America

Trans-Anglo Books
Box 2252, Main Station,
Los Angeles, California 90053

Trade Orders: P. O. Box 1771, Costa Mesa, California 92626

Locomotive No. 7, a Baldwin built in 1899, takes passengers by the hanging rocks at Clifton, high on the White Pass and Yukon Route. This scene on the narrow gauge was made in early Spring, 1900. (Dedman's Photo Shop)

Contents

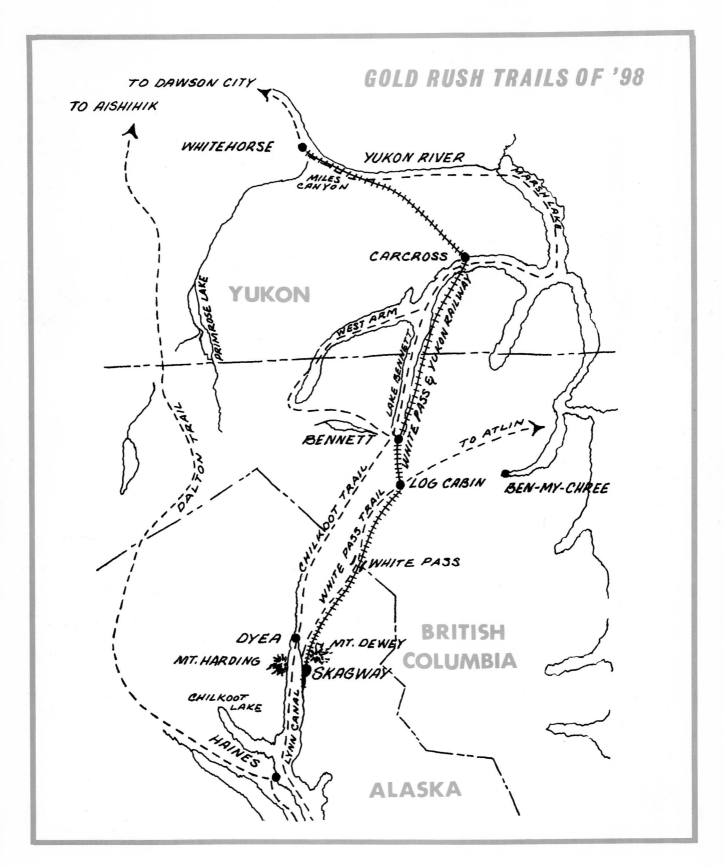

GOLD RUSH TRAILS OF '98

TO DAWSON CITY

TO AISHIHIK

WHITEHORSE

YUKON RIVER

MILES CANYON

MARSH LAKE

CARCROSS

YUKON

PRIMROSE LAKE

WEST ARM

LAKE BENNETT

WHITE PASS & YUKON RAILWAY

BENNETT

TO ATLIN

DALTON TRAIL

CHILKOOT TRAIL

WHITE PASS TRAIL

LOG CABIN

BEN-MY-CHREE

WHITE PASS

DYEA

MT. DEWEY

MT. HARDING

SKAGWAY

BRITISH COLUMBIA

CHILKOOT LAKE

LYNN CANAL

HAINES

ALASKA

This White Pass excursion train, which included an open coach, is pictured on Tunnel Mountain during the early 1900's. (Archives of Canada Photo)

Introduction

Contrary to the popular belief that narrow gauge railroading in North America is headquartered in Colorado, the continent's capital of "slim" railways can more logically be placed in the spectacularly beautiful country between Skagway, Alaska, and Whitehorse, Yukon Territory.

Here the 111.7-mile White Pass and Yukon Railway carries passengers and freight over a rugged but scenic route.

The narrow gauge conquers the St. Elias Mountains, a range not so high as it is rugged and steep. Sheer cliffs, long dark winters, and cold and snow blocked the way of the gold seekers of 1898 before the railway came. Even today the rugged country hasn't been conquered by a highway, but the three-foot gauge White Pass and Yukon — modern in its operations even though it preserves a heritage of Alaskan gold rush days — faithfully serves the area. It operates during the chilling winters as well as during the pleasant summers.

A Swedish emigrant, E. A. Hegg, photographed the White Pass during the pioneer gold rush era, using a dark room fastened to a sled pulled by a herd of long-haired goats. Hegg heated his developer to keep it from freezing and purified his water by filtering it through charcoal. Despite these difficulties, the pictures he made of the migration across the White Pass of the St. Elias Mountains became the most moving record of the Trail of 1898. This pioneer photographer made many of the pictures reproduced in this book.

The White Pass and Yukon Route was built as a gold rush railroad to ease the hardships of pioneers making the trek to the Klondike. The railway was operated by the U. S. Army during World War II, when it formed a vital supply link for the construction of the Alaska Highway. Today the narrow gauge carries freight for the growing Yukon Territory and caters to summer tourists.

The 111.7-mile narrow gauge is rich in memories of the Klondike gold rush. History is still intact at its two terminals, Skagway and Whitehorse. Open platform coaches, a 3.9 per cent grade, and way stations such as Log Cabin, Fraser, Bennett's, and Dead Horse Gulch make riding the three-foot gauge line a colorful experience.

Yet, the White Pass and Yukon Route is more than a memory of a picturesque era or a means to see spectacularly beautiful country. More than just a narrow gauge railway, it is a comprehensive transportation system which links the Yukon with Vancouver, British Columbia, and the "Lower Forty-eight" states. The modern, hard-working White Pass and Yukon supplies the safest and most economical access route to the far Northwest.

The W. P. & Y. — affectionately nicknamed "The Wait Patiently and You'll Ride" — by Alaska Pioneers — is moving into the 1970's carrying thousands of passengers.

During June, 1965, we shipped our car and ourselves southward over the White Pass from Whitehorse to Skagway. There in the old gateway to the Klondike we caught the Alaska Ferry System south. We returned to Skagway by ferry and rode the "White Pass" again during the summer of 1966.

The scenery was fabulous. The views of the Lynn Canal and the rugged St. Elias Mountains defy all description.

In the summer of 1964, we rode the Denver and Rio Grande Western's "Silverton" as it wound its way upward in Las Animas Canyon, Colorado. The brochure we received advertised it as "the last of the regularly scheduled narrow gauge trains in the United States." Such a statement was a little beyond truth, for as of January 3, 1959, Alaska attained statehood.

Incidentally, the Denver and Rio Grande

Western's narrow gauge trip covers only approximately forty-six miles between Silverton and Durango. The lesser known, but equally enjoyable, White Pass and Yukon Route, covers more than twice that distance.

It is easier to hop in a car and drive to southwestern Colorado than to make the trip to Alaska. Yet, the rides on the modern British Columbia and the Alaska Ferry systems are well worth the trip north. The rugged "inland passage" with its thousands of canals, channels, and islands is a return to the gold rush days. The "Klondikers" flocked north over the same waters.

At Skagway, near the Alaska Ferry dock, is a rambling frame building which serves as offices and depot for the White Pass Railway. The honk of the air horn on the modern General Electric C-C diesel announces the departure of train No. 1, northbound to Whitehorse. The consist is a mixed string of historically old arch-bar trucked parlor cars, tankers, and modern container loaded flats. Frequently, an open platform combine with a cupola brings up the rear of the daily mixed.

Cars and highway buses ride on flat cars during the summer months. Tourists in cars and campers head north by rail every day.

This is a portrayal of the history of the White Pass and Yukon Route and its relationships to the Great Gold Rush of 1898. It is hoped it will be read by tourists, general readers, and rail fans alike. Some of the tragedy, heroism, humor, determination, and hope of the early northern pioneers are expressed on these pages.

The author wishes to thank Roy Minter and Carl E. Mulvihill of the White Pass and Yukon Route for their help and source material. The Provincial Archives of British Columbia, Dedman's Photo Shop, The Canadian Government Travel and Publicity Bureau, and the Alaska Travel Division all helped supply the historic photographs. The author especially wishes to thank his wife for her typing, proofreading, patience, and criticism of the manuscript.

CY MARTIN

This dramatic 1898 gold rush scene was at Newman, on the dreaded "Dead Horse Trail" north of Skagway. (Provincial Archives of British Columbia)

Hell Trail to Gold

CHAPTER I

In the spring of 1896 George Carmack and two Indian friends, Skookum Jim and Dawson Charley, were scouting around on Bonanza Creek just south of the Klondike River Valley. The bottom of the creek yielded a few flakes of gold — barely enough, in fact, to fill a spent cartridge case. Yet, the discovery triggered the great Klondike Gold Rush.

The call of riches lured thousands of prospectors who wrote a stirring chapter in Alaskan history. The thrilling times yielded millions of dollars in gold and, incidentally, resulted in building the White Pass and Yukon Railway, a picturesque narrow gauge that conquered rugged country.

Aghast at the wild hordes of gold seekers, a United States marshal on the scene remarked that "the like had never been known. Never would it be seen again."

While most of the world's frontiers commanded similar enthusiastic rhetoric, the marshal's words proved an understatement as far as the Klondike was concerned. Most gold rushes are unbelievable. The Klondike was the most unbelievable gold rush of them all.

Inadequate transportation plagued the enthusiasts who wanted to join the trek to the gold fields. Of every four fortune hunters that set out from the south to reach the Klondike, three gave up en route. The way was rugged. The average gold seeker boarded a crowded steamer in Seattle or Vancouver and travelled approximately a thousand miles up the Inland Passage to Skagway or nearby Dyea. From there, would-be prospectors could choose to reach the Yukon by hiking forty-five miles over 2,400-foot White Pass or 3,500-foot Chilkoot Pass.

Assuming that his horse didn't die during the arduous crossing through the mountains and that he still had funds after buying costly provisions, the gold-seeker continued the difficult journey. He would leave the mountain trail, build a raft, and navigate more than 500 miles down the Yukon River to the gold fields near Dawson City. The journey there from Seattle required at least ninety days.

Sometimes it took a year!

When the dream of the Klondike ended, Daw-

Pioneer photographer E. A. Hegg recorded prospectors struggling over Chilkoot Pass through the snow in 1898. (Provincial Archives of British Columbia)

son went into hibernation. A few of the pioneer landmarks disappeared, one by one, in disasters of fire or through man's callousness. The hills, the creeks, and the picturesque names — the names like Bonanza, Hunger, Klondike, Dome, Dawson, and the Palace Grand — are there today.

The White Pass and Yukon Railway was completed just about the time Dawson City completed its hour on the stage of history. The narrow gauge remains as a living legend of the past.

The railway was never a part of the official historic heritage. It built and rebuilt itself.

Characters such as George Carmack, Skookum Jim, Dawson Jake, and Arizona Charley would feel right at home today on the red plush seats of the arch-bar trucked combination cars still running. Coatless Curley Monroe, Hamgrease Jimmy, Diamond Toothed Gurty, Nellie the Pig, and "Klondike Kate" Rockwell all rode on the rails of the White Pass Route.

The Golden Spike ceremony at Carcross, Yukon Territory, on July 29, 1900, marked the completion of the White Pass Railway. It also marked the end of the Klondike gold rush. Prospectors and dancing girls, the captains of commerce, and the hangers-on left for greener pastures. They left to pursue their search for riches on the beaches at Nome.

The exodus was not the end of the railroad and it did not end the life of Dawson City. It started a restful period following a hectic beginning. The gold rush produced a strange insanity of plague-like proportions. An "army" of gold seekers 30,000 to 40,000 strong invaded the north in a frantic search for riches. These people, eighty per cent of whom came from the United States, provided the real beginnings for Skagway, Whitehorse, and the Yukon.

Prior to the gold rush of 1898 the Yukon was little more than an abstract spot on a map. For most people, it was as remote as the isolated islands of the Arctic Sea. It attracted a few prospectors pursuing their searchings for gold. An occasional trader or itinerant missionary made the trek to the area, and of course there were, the red-coated Canadian "Mounties." Aside from these lonely people, there were few signs of civilization.

In 1896, before the gold rush started, approximately 1,700 prospectors panned $300,000 worth of gold. In 1900, with the rush well under way, the population of the Yukon Valley had soared to more than 50,000. The value of gold production skyrocketed to $22 million.

a few over-burdened coastal steamers until the vessels bulged with the eager men. The lure of gold magically beckoned them northward.

How did the gold rush begin? Who actually made the dramatic discovery of the precious metal? Whose pan first brought up so many nuggets from the water? Old-timers hotly debated these questions for years.

No single incident comparable to the finding of gold at Sutter's Mill in California marked the beginning of the rush in Alaska. Instead, two legends developed. One involved Bob Hender-

E. A. Hegg also made this photograph of a prospector on "Dead Horse" or White Pass Trail in Summer, 1898. (Provincial Archives of British Columbia)

The mad stampede of 1898 and 1899 rippled like a tidal wave through Canada and the United States. Gold Fever was rampant. But three out of every four who started the trek to the Yukon quit along the way because of obstacles to travel. The trail was long and the Northland was jealous of her golden horde. Thousands of black-suited, bowler-hatted gold seekers gathered on the docks of Vancouver, San Francisco, Seattle, and Victoria to seek passage to the north. They tried to crowd aboard

son and the other pertained to George Carmack. The Indians, Skookum Jim and Tagish Charley, who were with Carmack, each gave versions of what happened.

Probably the best answers as to how the gold rush started come from William Ogilvie, the pioneer who later described the era in a book.

"In August, 1896," reported Ogilvie, "the world startling discovery of the Klondike was made which for a year or two put a period to all exploration and prospecting except in the

This photo, made in the Fall of 1898, shows the settlement that was developing in White Pass to serve those struggling over the rugged terrain to the gold fields. (H. Pollard Collection from the Provincial Archives of Alberta)

immediate vicinity.

"To discover the true origin of the gold rush," Ogilvie continued, "we should go back a year or two in history. Robert Henderson was prospecting along Hunger Creek and Indian River during the winter of 1894 and 1895. He returned to the little trading post at Ogilvie to replenish his rations and tried to find a partner to help relieve the loneliness. On his way back, at the mouth of Klondike, he met George Washington Carmack. According to the unwritten code, Henderson told him of the discovery he had made on Gold Bottom. Henderson invited

Carmack to come up and stay, but Carmack was engaged with salmon fishing with his Indian friends, Skookum Jim and Tagish Charley."

Henderson strongly objected to the Indians. He didn't want his creek staked by natives, especially ones from the Upper River. Carmack was offended and they parted company. Carmack and his Indian friends camped at the mouth of the Klondike while fishing, but grew tired of the monotonous fish diet.

To obtain money for food, they decided to cut logs and take them down to Forty Mile to sell at the saw mill. While working, they panned some of the gravel along the river bottom.

"As to exactly who made the true discovery of the bonanza," Ogilvie recalled, "there is considerable discrepancy. Each, Carmack, Tagish Charley, and Skookum Jim claimed to have panned the first color. No matter what, the gold was put into a Winchester rifle cartridge and the party went on to the mouth of the Klondike.

"They prepared a small raft of logs and Carmack and Charley floated down on it. When Carmack and Tagish Charley reached Forty Mile they told of the discovery, but only a few paid much attention. Carmack was known as a 'Squaw Man' and didn't follow mining as a business. Oh, he had prospected some, but he wasn't well known. Also, his association with the Indians created a strong prejudice against him."

Carmack and his party "staked" on August 19, 1896. Two days later Edward Monahan and Gregg Stewart staked claims. The following day E. Edwards, J. Moffat, Robertson, and Kimball staked their claims. They were old mining hands and their word was believed. The rush was on!

Bob Henderson bitterly resented Carmack's failure to send him any word of the discovery. Henderson didn't learn of it until after all the ground on both Bonanza and Eldorado Creeks was thoroughly claimed. Most of the men who filed claims were old-timers. They had sunk shafts and shoveled gravel on creek after creek along the Yukon without finding bonanzas. No one really believed this was the richest placer creek in the world.

Almost every claim from No. 1 through No. 40 was worth at least a half million dollars. Some were worth three times that amount!

Word spread and new arrivals found a tent town stretched out along the bank of the Yukon at the Klondike's mouth. The city of Dawson grew during the winter of '96 and '97. No one on the outside knew of the camp or of the gold nourishing it. All through the long dark winter, the prospectors worked, reaping a rich harvest of gold dust and nuggets. It was dream-like in its unreality. The miners watched in fascina-

The riches of the Klondike were fabled. These men were returning from the gold fields on the S. S. City of Topeka as millionaires. (Provincial Archives of British Columbia)

tion and disbelief when more and more gold accumulated in their fruit jars, bottles, Bull Durham sacks, or moose-skin pouches. Fortune was making a game of them. There was plenty of gold, but it was worthless in the far-north settlement of Dawson City.

Spring came at last and down the Yukon puffed the *Portus B. Wear* and the ungainly *Alice* on a 1,700 mile voyage to the sea. On board the two little river steamers there was gold in suitcases, gold in boxes, gold in packing cases, gold in belts, and gold in pokes of caribou hide. Gold was in jam jars, medicine bottles, and tomato cans. Gold was stacked on the decks and in the purser's cabin.

A total of three tons of gold and eighty prospectors went aboard the two little boats. When the two steamers reached the mud flats of St. Michael, the newly rich Klondike millionaires boarded the rusty steamers *Portland*, and the *Excelsior*, the former headed for Seattle and other for San Francisco.

The *Excelsior* reached San Francisco on July 15, 1897, but the *Portland*, even though it had a shorter distance to travel, didn't reach Seattle until two days later.

Conditions were exactly right for the lunacy which followed. The world was at peace and the Klondike had no rival for the public's attention. The Yukon was just far enough away

Alaska's Other Railroad

BY THE EDITORS OF
TRANS-ANGLO BOOKS

□

Alaska's other railroad begins approximately four hundred and fifty miles northwest of Skagway and unlike the White Pass and Yukon is a standard gauge (4'8½") system.

This railway is the Alaska Railroad, with a 470-mile main line stretching from Seward to Fairbanks, metropolis of the state's interior. The railroad embraces a total of approximately five hundred and forty miles.

The railway, owned and operated by the United States government, is administered by the Department of the Interior.

The privately-financed Alaskan Central Railway went bankrupt in the early twentieth century because of the heavy cost of construction through the rugged mountains. The fact that Alaska had been developed so little offered no returns to venture capital in the foreseeable future, and there were no takers to resume construction of the financially-troubled line.

Uncle Sam stepped in.

Congress in 1914 appropriated $35 million — nearly five times the price paid Russia in 1867 for all Alaska — to build the railway. Work started in 1915. The rugged terrain and cold climate produced ordeals for the builders. The railway cost $56 million to construct and was completed in 1923. President Warren G. Harding drove a gold spike for the official opening of the Alaska Railroad.

While the railroad has performed well in developing and serving Alaska, it has never been profitable. Operating costs have been high and business for the line has been as sparse as the population of the area it serves. The government has picked up the tab for the losses.

Despite its financial losses, the railroad is regarded as important to the economy by Alaskans who otherwise would have to fight highways made difficult by the terrain and climate.

The line itself is responsible for the establishment of at least two major cities in Alaska. Seward, on Resurrection Bay off the Gulf of Alaska, was founded in 1902 as the base of operations for the railroaders whose plans were stopped by bankruptcy. The city of Anchorage on Cook Inlet was founded in 1915 as headquarters for building the government railroad.

Both cities have grown and prospered as Alaska developed.

Steep grades distinguish the Alaska Railroad, although its grades are not so abrupt as those on the White Pass and Yukon. The first fifty miles provide the steepest grades: they range from 1.5 to 2.2 per cent, as compared to up to 3.9 per cent on the narrow gauge.

Spectacular bridges help make the line noteworthy north of Anchorage. The railroad crosses the Susitna River, approximately one hundred and fifty miles from Anchorage, with approximately 1,300 feet of spans. A steel arch bridge 900 feet long bridges Hurricane Gulch.

Here is the mileage report on the Alaska Railroad:

    0 Seward
114.3 Anchorage
248.5 Curry
347.9 McKinley Park
358.1 Healy
411.7 Nenana
470.3 Fairbanks

The Alaska Railroad became an important defense link during World War II, and like the White Pass and Yukon helped haul men and materials for building the Alaska Highway, which terminates at Fairbanks.

Like the White Pass, the Alaska Railroad promises to be an attraction for rail fans and other travelers well into the 1970's.

The Alaska Railroad, which unlike the W. P. & Y. R. uses standard gauge (4'8½") tracks, provides service for an important area of the state north of Skagway. These pictures show the line in operation during the 1960's. (Photo: Jess Adams-Alaska-Yukon Railroad Historical Society, Inc.)

Tame goats brought from Oregon hauled freight to the Klondike gold fields and then were fattened and slaughtered for food. (Public Archives of Canada)

to be romantic and just close enough to be accessible. Rich men could travel all the way by boat. Poor men could reach the mountain passes, cross them by foot, and float on a homemade raft down the fast flowing Yukon to the gold fields.

The Pacific Coast ports hungered for trade and the merchants used every weapon to promote their city as the outfitting port for the Stampede of '98. The gold rush gathered momentum swiftly in the late summer months. By mid-winter the great stampede was moving at express-train speed.

It was estimated that more than a million people laid plans to leave homes and families to seek fortunes in the bonanza of the North. At least 100,000 actually set out on the long journey to the gold fields on the Yukon.

Virtually every train traveling across the continent boasted a "gold rush car." The walls were lined with glass jars of nuggets and dust and papered with photographs of the Klondike. Books, maps, and pamphlets of interest to the gold seekers cluttered cabinets and tables. The fare from Chicago to the Pacific Coast dropped to $10.

While the railroads obligingly dropped fares, the operators of ships profited from the mass movement northward. During the fall of 1897 steamship tickets sold at fantastically high prices. Before the *Excelsior* left on the return voyage to St. Michael, her agents turned away more than ten times the number of people she could carry. As the fall progressed and winter began, a grotesque flotilla of oddly assorted craft shuttled up and down the Pacific coast, crammed with stampeders bound for Skagway, Dyea, Wrangell, or St. Michael.

To those on the west coast there was only one way to the Klondike, and that was by the sea. Shipping men combed the ship boneyards from Southern California to Vancouver in search of anything that would float. Many vessels blundered about the channels without compasses or experienced crews, finally striking a hidden rock and sinking beneath the waves with all hands lost.

A tugboat company dispatched the *Sea Lion* north towing two barges, *A-Jax* and *B-Jax*, both crammed with a mass of freight and passengers. The *Richard Holyoak* towed the river sternwheeler *W. H. Merwin* all the way to Alaska with a full load of passengers sealed up in the latter's boxed-in cabin.

The 45-foot steam launch *Rustler*, commanded by a former San Francisco milk-wagon driver, made it to Skagway with seventy passengers. The ship was licensed to carry twenty-five on the placid waters of San Francisco Bay.

It was a colorful armada that sailed the Salt water section of the Trail of 1898.

Space was at a premium, as one unnamed passenger aboard the *Amur* described it: "A floating bedlam, pandemonium let loose, Black Hole of Calcutta in an Arctic setting."

The *Amur* normally carried one hundred passengers. On this trip its owner crammed five hundred aboard together with dogs of all breeds. Included in the passenger list were fifty prostitutes, stacked ten to a cabin. There were only three berths in a room and a girl each pounced on a bunk as soon as it was vacated and slept with her clothes on whenever the opportunity arose. The *Amur's* dining room accommodated twenty-six people at a sitting. Every meal took seven hours to serve. By the time they reached Skagway, the passengers were famished.

Skagway, the "Gateway to the Klondike," was founded by William Moore, who in 1888 built a cabin at the foot of White Pass, on the delta of the Skagway River where it rushes eagerly into the sea. The name was derived from the Indian word *Skagus,* or "home of the north wind."

The first seventy-four years in Captain William Moore's life were crammed with enough adventure and drama to fill a dozen books. At the time of the gold rush, the white-bearded ex-steamship captain was dreaming of his newest enterprise, building a boom town at the head of Skagway Bay.

Captain Moore thought there would be a gold rush to the Yukon valleys long before George Carmack made his strike on the Klondike. He believed that the main body of stampeders would come up the narrow Lynn Canal and across the pass he earlier had discovered in the St. Elias Mountains.

He named this discovery "White Pass," honoring Sir Thomas White, the Canadian Minister of the Interior.

The discovery came after the ex-captain heard reports of a pass in the coast mountains not far from the steep and dangerous Chilkoot Pass. Assisted by his friend, William Ogilvie, and an Indian, Snookum Jim, Captain Moore

Royal Mail Stage No. 1 was typical of coaches used between rail heads before completion of the narrow gauge. (Provincial Archives of British Columbia)

excitedly surveyed the pass. He was pleased to note that the newly-discovered pass was low enough for pack animals to use.

The trail through White Pass stretched twenty-five miles, ten miles more than via the Dyea or Chilkoot Trail. The fact that it was six hundred feet lower than the other trail gave the White Pass route an advantage. The zig-zagging, roller coaster switch-back route through hills, canyons, mountains, and valleys was suitable in good conditions for travel by pack horse, ox, mule, dog, or goat.

Old Captain Moore saw its possibilities at once and in 1888 he built his cabin at the foot of White Pass on the delta where the river rushed on its way to spending itself on the wooded flat at the head of Skagway Bay on the Lynn Canal.

Moore lived like a monarch in that lonely area. The only other cabin in the district was a small trading post established by John Healy on a neighboring inlet.

On July 26, 1897, the first gold rush steamer anchored in Skagway Bay and dumped its load of kicking horses, yelping dogs, scrambling men, and loose women into the shallow waters. They invaded Moore's small domain.

They poured ashore like a conquering horde, paying little attention to the protesting old man. It was as if he were one of the trees they slashed down to make room for their tents and shacks. They heaped their supplies and goods

Snow virtually buried the White Pass Hotel, in center, when E. A. Hegg made this photograph in February, 1899. The partially completed White Pass railroad is high on the mountainside in distance. (Public Archives of Canada)

on the beach, and tethered their animals in the forest. They burned, hacked, and gouged away at the beautiful wooded delta and a rough semblance of a town emerged.

Skagway was born!

Ship after ship spewed its human cargo on the beach. By August 12, the residents established a local government and chose a committee to lay out a town. Frank Reid, an ex-school teacher and Indian fighter, was appointed town surveyor.

The town of Skagway was conceived in lawlessness and nurtured in murder and thievery.

Of all the routes to the Klondike gold fields, the "Dead Horse" trail across White Pass brought out the worst in a man. No one who survived ever forgot and most who recalled their days on the trail did so with a sense of shame and remorse. The White Pass trail looked easy, unlike the Chilkoot Trail from Dyea that led directly to the base of the Pass and then, in a single leap called the "Staircase," spanned the mountain barrier.

By contrast, the White Pass at first glance seemed little more than a jaunt through the rolling hills on horseback.

Yet, the terrain was so cruel that many men crossing the pass were seized by a delirium driving them to the pit of insanity and into primitive brutality.

The White Pass route — or "Dead Horse" Trail as it was aptly called — from Skagway crossed a series of obstacles. It began as an attractive wagon road leading for a few miles over flat timber land and through a small swamp. Then the Dead Horse Trail started a series of precipitous climbs. An almost impassable mire of soggy marsh, the Skagway River bed, separated each hill from the next. The trail then zig-zagged via a narrow pathway along the sheer cliffs of the mountains.

Devil's Hill, with slippery slate, had a path scarcely two feet wide. The pathway wound like a corkscrew where a single misstep of the loaded horse would mean death on the rocks, five hundred feet below. Porcupine Hill, next, was a sort of roller coaster affair where the wretched foot-sore horses picked their way between ten-foot boulders.

Samuel H. Graves, president of the White Pass Railway that eventually was to conquer the treacherous route, rode up the Dead Horse Trail before the line was built. On the way to the summit he passed a horse with a broken leg.

"This was at a point where the trail squeezed between two large boulders," he recalled later. "The horse's pack was removed and someone had knocked it in head with an axe, mercifully killing it. Traffic on the trail was resumed directly across the still-warm body of the horse."

Graves returned to the point toward dusk.

"There wasn't a vestige of the carcass left," he reported. "The head was on one side of the trail and the tail on the other. The beast was ground into the earth by the trampling feet of the human machine as it fought its way toward the gold fields of the Klondike."

Major J. M. Walsh, of the Northwest Mounted Police, described the Dead Horse Trail as "a scene of havoc and destruction — one beyond all imagination.

"Thousands of pack horses lie dead along the way, sometimes in bunches under the

River boats were docked near the W. P. & Y. station in this view of Bennett, B. C., during booming August, 1899. (Provincial Archives of British Columbia)

cliffs," he said, "with pack-saddles and packs where they have fallen from the rock above, sometimes in tangled masses filling the mud holes and furnishing the only footing for our poor pack animals on the march — often, I regret to say, exhausted but still alive, a fact that we are unaware of until after the miserable wretches turn beneath the hoofs of our cavalcade. The eyeless sockets of the pack animals everywhere account for the myriads of ravens along the road. The inhumanity which this trail has been witness to, the heartbreak and suffering that so many have undergone, cannot be imagined. They certainly cannot be described."

Jack London, who won fame as a writer during the era, also saw the tragedy that befell the horses.

"Horses died like mosquitoes in the first frost and from Skagway to Bennett they lay rotted in heaps," he wrote in *Tales of the Klondike and Yukon*.

"They died at the rocks, they were poisoned at the summit, and they starved at the lakes,"

The improvised White Pass Hotel, pictured in the Spring of 1898, was a stopping place on the Dead Horse Trail. (Public Archives of British Columbia)

London continued. "They fell off the trail, what there was of it, and they went through it; in the river they drowned under their load or were smashed to pieces against the boulders; they snapped their legs in crevasses and broke their backs falling backwards with their packs; in the sloughs they sank from fright or smothered in the slime; they were disemboweled in the bogs where the corduroy logs turned end up in the mud; men shot them, worked them to death, and when they were gone, went back to the beach and bought more. Some did not bother to shoot them. Stripping their saddles off and their shoes and leaving them where they fell."

At last came the climb to summit, a thousand foot rise in less than a mile!

During the summer, liquid mud streamed down the path in rivulets. Sharp jagged rocks tore at the horses' feet and flanks. Slabs of fallen granite barred the way. Yawning mud holes swallowed the floundering animals, packs and all.

The summit of White Pass was the border between Canada and Alaska, but it was not the end of the "Hell Trail." The slender trail skirted a net-work of glacial lakes, crossed Tunnel Mountain, and finally descended in the Tutshi Valley. One more low pass remained before reaching Lake Bennett and the headwaters of the Yukon River. The summit, called "Log Cabin," became the site of a fair sized town. The Northwest Mounted Police headquartered there. It later became the start of the Fan Tail

Trail to the Atlin gold fields.

Nearly 5,000 men and women tried to cross White Pass in the fall of 1897. Only a tiny handful reached Bennett's in time to navigate the Yukon River before the winter freeze-up. One "Klondiker" who succeeded compared the slow movement of men and supplies over the pass to an army in retreat. On the coastal side of the pass, a constant gray drizzle of rain shut out the sunlight and produced the streams of mud and gumbo that nearly stopped all movement.

The trail was so narrow that it wouldn't allow two horses to pass. Time and time again all movement ground to a stop. The wretched horses, for miles and miles back, stood with crushing loads pressing down on their backs. An animal would remain loaded for twenty-four hours with no rest or respite from the heavy pack. More than 3,000 horses went into service in the fall of 1897. Scarcely a handful survived the grueling trip across White Pass.

Many of the doomed beasts were ready for the glue factory when bought in Victoria, Seattle, Portland, or San Francisco. They were literally thrown off the deck of steamers into Skagway Bay, where they were purchased by eager men who never handled animals before. Often two partners would spend a whole day trying to load a single horse. At Summit, horses which cost $200 in Skagway were worth less than 20 cents.

Along the trail, the horses died. From Skagway to Bennett their corpses rotted in heaps. Most owners did not bother to shoot the fallen or crippled horses. They stripped off the saddles and the shoes and left them where they fell.

Along the "Dead Horse" Trail, the Klondiker's hearts were cold and hard as the granite of the St. Elias Mountains.

By the middle of September, all movement along Dead Horse Trail came to a standstill. No one would reach the Klondike until the following spring. Thousands retreated and tried to sell their outfits. Nobody wanted them, so outfits were strewn along the route for more than forty miles. The tidal flats at Skagway grew black with horses, men, and supplies. Everywhere the pall of gloom hung over the gold rush.

A lucky few reached Lake Bennett, built rafts or boats, and floated down the mighty Yukon to the heart of the Klondike gold fields at Dawson City. They felt secure in the knowledge of winning. They held the lead while others faltered along the way. They traveled light and ignored the advice to take provisions. They had money and expected to make more money panning gold. After all, they reasoned, with money, you can buy anything.

But there was no food in Dawson City. In vain, these "Winning" Klondikers offered bank notes for food, but their money was useless. Thousands were racing to reach Dawson. But in Dawson itself, the old timers were abandoning the town. There was no food. Gold was everywhere, but it would buy little during the winter of 1897-98.

When April finally came, a few hardy souls with dog teams came from Dyea and Skagway with food for sale. They didn't bring staples. Instead they brought a rare collection of luxuries — tins of oysters, turkey, and eggs. Tinned milk sold for $1 a can.

On June 8 the mighty Yukon River came alive with boats. They poured into Dawson City day and night in an endless parade. The first steam boat arrived with sixteen barrels of whiskey. It went on sale immediately at $1 in gold dust a shot. The famine in Dawson was over. The long and arduous route to the Klondike took its toll. The enormous influx of Klondikers demanded the development of some relatively easy form of transportation.

The long all-water route to St. Michael and up the Yukon by paddle-wheel steamer was too slow. The Chilkoot and White Pass trails were virtually impassable during winters. Sledding down the Yukon was impossible. Only during the brief summer months could supplies and goods be brought down stream from the headwaters at Lake Bennett past the Whitehorse rapids and into Dawson City.

The great gold rush brought a boom to the North. There was a desperate need for reliable

Modern day Skagway is distinguished by many picturesque buildings remaining from gold rush days. This view is on Broadway. (Dedman's Photo Shop, Skagway)

shipping methods between the booming town of Dawson and the outside world. To those on the West Coast, there was only one way to the Klondike, and this was by the Inland Passage to Skagway at the head of the Lynn Canal, over the White Pass and down the mighty Yukon to Dawson. Steamers could carry the tons of freight and food stuffs to Dawson City from the new town of Whitehorse at the foot of the rapids of the Yukon River. The one hundred and ten miles from Skagway to Whitehorse must be crossed by a wagon road or railroad.

This illustration depicts an 1898 gambling hall in booming Skagway. The gold rush attracted fortune seekers from many nations. (Dedman's Photo Shop)

Rails over White Pass

CHAPTER II

Dawson City and the Klondike obviously would need a permanent and well-organized transportation system. This was clear from the start. The first man to ease the journey from Skagway north over the White Pass was Sylvester Schoville of Joseph Pulitzer's famous newspaper, the New York *World*. Late in the Fall of 1897, Schoville offered on behalf of his paper, the princely sum of $2,000 to pay for dynamiting narrow sections along the White Pass Trail.

Schoville, accompanied by his recent bride, arrived in Skagway wearing a dashing costume of high leather boots, tight corduroys, and a white sombrero. He even brought his guitar along to entertain the Klondikers. His offer was too generous for the *World*. The newspaper refused to go along with the scheme and immediately recalled him to New York. Before leaving the area, Schoville did widen a small section of the trail. He hired twelve men at $450 a day to guard this section and collect toll, but

they couldn't hold back the press of 3,000 men anxious to reach the gold fields.

The next person seeking to improve travel was George Brackett, ex-mayor of Minneapolis, who started construction of a wagon road along the mountain sides of the White Pass. Brackett lost his first fortune in the panic of 1893 and was anxious to recoup the loss. In the early fall of 1897, he tramped up to the pass in the St. Elias Mountains, 2,885 feet above sea level. Convinced that a toll wagon road would solve transportation problems, Brackett sank $185,000 of his own money into the project.

He blew off some offending rock spurs, using more than four hundred tons of dynamite and black powder. Despite such adventures as calling for the U. S. troops to discipline the prospectors for evading his toll keepers, he finally finished the project. His wagon road was a minor success. The stampeders gladly paid the

E. A. Hegg made this dramatic photograph on August 6, 1898, on Porcupine Hill. Laborers were laying the railway over the rugged wagon road, previously the only way to cross forbidding White Pass. (Public Archives of Canada)

tolls during the winter months of 1897 and 1898.

The ghosts of the dead horses on the old trail below undoubtedly haunted each Klondiker passing along the route.

Thanks to the new road, freight rates over the White Pass dropped from 75 cents to 12 cents a pound.

Frank Leslie's Monthly, a popular journal of the era, proclaimed:

"The isolation of Alaska was at an end."

A chance meeting of two imaginative and colorful men early in 1898 solved the problem of good transportation. Both men were independently investigating the possibility of building a narrow-gauge railroad from Skagway to Whitehorse.

One of the individuals was Sir Thomas Tancrede, representing a group of British financiers who wanted to finance a railway. The other man was Michael J. Henry, a Canadian railway contractor who was nicknamed the "Irish Prince."

When Sir Thomas arrived, he looked aghast at rugged White Pass. He decided that a railway could never be built over such forbidding terrain and advised his backers in Great Britain that they make investments elsewhere.

The Briton concluded that the mountains were too massive and that the sheer walls would make grades too steep for a railroad. The route from the sea level to the summit would be along virtually sheer cliff walls and the white hell of the area's winters would add to the prob-. lems. Sir Thomas decided that the project of building a railway over the terrain was beyond the ability of any engineer.

In Skagway he met Mike Heney by chance at a bar. Michael J. Heney had returned to Skagway after making an independent examination of the area. The White Pass and rugged St. Elias Mountains did not faze him. He believed a railroad could be constructed across the mountain range to Whitehorse. He was also thoroughly convinced he was the only man in the world who could do it.

Mike Heney was sure steel rails three feet apart could be laid from sea level to 2,800 feet in twenty miles. But, it would take money. "Big Mike" Heney and Sir Thomas Tancrede looked each other over and each recognized likeable qualities in the other. They became friends immediately and soon tackled the problems of building the railroad through the toughest country in North America. The pair talked far into the night and by early morning the construction of the railroad was no longer an impossible dream. It was an accepted challenge. It would demand everything Big Mike Heney could offer.

The White Pass and Yukon Railway was organized in the spring of 1898, and among its first acts was the purchase of George Brackett's wagon road. Brackett knew the difficulties that he faced with labor and construction as well as the political problems of dealing with three separate governments—the American, the Canadian, and the Provincial Government of British Columbia. There were no accurate boundary surveys between Canada and Alaska. Brackett recognized that he couldn't deal with the exasperatingly slow and frustrating problems. He readily accepted the offer and turned all of his construction equipment over to Heney and Sir Thomas.

The Canadian Senate rejected a House of

Laborers, their faces showing varying emotions, paused to pose for this picture while building the narrow gauge at Lake Bennett. (Alaska Travel Bureau)

Commons bill early in 1898 for a franchise to McKenzie and Mann to build an all-Canadian railway from the Stikene River to Teslin Lake. The legislators felt the White Pass railway offered the only feasible solution for the transportation problem hindering the development of the Klondike. The British capitalists, under the able leadership of Sir Thomas Tancrede, negotiated and obtained charters from Washing, Ottawa, and Victoria. Now Big Mike's plans to build the narrow gauge railway from Skagway to Whitehorse were government approved. The original plan called for laying track from Skagway Harbor to Whitehorse and on north to Fort Selkirk, a distance of more than three hundred and twenty-five miles.

Officials of the Whitehorse and Yukon line chose a width of three feet between rails for their track. This labelled the railway as a "narrow gauge" road, since most contemporary lines were adopting the "standard" gauge of four feet eight and one-half inches between rails so that the rolling stock of different companies could be interchanged.

25

Undaunted by cold weather, these workmen were erecting a railroad bridge near the White Pass summit in the Winter of 1898-99. (Public Archives of Canada)

Incidentally, only during the late nineteenth century were American railroads agreeing on a "standard" gauge for tracks. The Erie Railroad originally was built with a six-foot gauge. Until 1886, a five-foot gauge was "standard" for railroads in the South.

The three-foot gauge railway achieved its most notable fame with the building of the narrow gauge Denver and Rio Grande through the rugged Rocky Mountains. There, construction costs would have risen considerably if the wider "standard" gauge were used. Advocates

of narrow gauge railroads noted substantial savings were possible through construction of a ten-foot road bed instead of the fifteen feet required for standard gauge tracks. Such proponents also noted that more savings were realized through a narrow gauge's use of lighter rails and coaches.

The builders of the White Pass and Yukon Route noted that construction costs through the steep and rocky White Pass would be reduced considerably by building a narrow gauge line. Cutting a right-of-way along the sheer cliffs would be an expensive proposition even for a narrow gauge railway. A standard gauge railway would skyrocket costs even higher.

Completion of a narrow gauge railway over rugged White Pass, with its forbidding weather, would solve the area's transportation problems. The builders recognized that the possibility of interchange of cars with any other railway indeed was remote in that isolated area so lacking in adequate transportation.

Soapy Smith, head of Skagway's lawless element, posed for this photo in the early 1890's while in Colorado. (Denver Public Library Western Collection)

When construction started, the White Pass and Yukon builders encountered problems in getting materials. Confusion reigned over shipping any kind of supplies to the area. Prospectors and railway men fought for the meager space that was available. Shipments — including the Klondikers with their dogs, tents, and supplies, along with the railway construction equipment and material — landed together in the sea of mud on the beach at Skagway.

The railroad's first shipload of horses, rail, ties, and spikes — and laborers to do the work — was unloaded at Skagway on May 27, 1898. The very next morning, laborers began laying track up Broadway, Skagway's main street. The track aimed straight north to the White Pass notch in the St. Elias Mountains.

Not long after starting work, the new company found its first delay-causing troubles. After buying Brackett's interest in the toll road, engineers made five surveys of different routes to determine the best right-of-way over the forty miles to Lake Bennett. They ended by using the same pass discovered and named by Captain William Moore. They found a "false pass" and a so-called "warm pass," but neither were satisfactory. Dead Horse Trail remained the best route.

Customs problems plagued the railroad as well as the sourdoughs. There was a major difference of opinion as to the exact location of the Alaska-Canada border. The Canadian Northwest Mounted Police thought Skagway was in Canada and established headquarters there. The American officials settled comfortably at Log Cabin, thirty miles to the north.

But the thing that interfered with building the railway was the lawlessness of Skagway.

A bearded character known as "Soapy" Smith led the community's lawless element. Jefferson Randolph Smith regarded the Klondike gold fields as the golden opportunity to utilize his illegal talents. Born in Georgia to respectable parents, Soapy drifted to the mining camps of the West. Soon he was well-known in Denver, Creede, Leadville, and Central City. These mining camps knew him as a personable young man, an expert in manipulating the pea and shell game, and a high-pressure salesman for soap.

In his youth, Soapy followed the circuses and carnivals. There, standing on a wooden box in full view of the crowd, he would wrap crisp new five dollar bills around cakes of Castile soap, replace the regular wrapper, and give his "come-on" pitch.

The speech extolled all the virtues of his fine Castile soap. The "capper" was a young man in the audience who would rush up and buy a cake of soap. This was always a "loaded" cake, and the "capper" would wave his bill and shout excitedly. When the customers rushed to buy, they failed to profit. Their cakes of soap failed to yield five dollar bills. When the crowd became restless, Soapy would quickly move on and set up shop at another spot. This earned him the name "Soapy," and he proudly held it throughout his short and tempestious life.

Early in the fall of 1897, Soapy slowly worked his way up the coast from Seattle. He landed first at Dyea and then moved to Skagway. Soapy decided to stake this boom town at the head of the Lynn Canal as his claim for gold mining. A born leader and a good mixer, he soon recruited a gang of gamblers, thugs, and pickpockets. Many of them were his former friends from down south in the gold towns of Colorado.

The nucleus of Soapy's new gang included the "Reverend" Charles Bowers, Syd Dixon, George Wilder, "Slim Jim" Foster, and "Red" Gibbs. This hard core of crooks soon dominated Skagway. Smith planned with care and charted the ground meticulously. Before settling definitely in Skagway, he wandered up and down the panhandle of Alaska. He discarded Wrangell, Juneau, and Ketchikan. He rejected Dyea because the Chilkoot Trail was open all the year. It was the White Pass Trail, open only part of the year, which attracted him, Skagway was the bottle-neck. Gold seekers bound for the Klondike always filled Skagway. He never dreamed that a railroad could change this and cause his downfall.

The gang settled in Skagway, with headquarters in a saloon and gambling hall known as "Jeff's Oyster Palace."

The gang did not prey on the permanent citizens. Instead, Soapy curried favor with

Soapy Smith's notorious "parlor" became an attraction for tourists in Skagway. (Dedman's Photo Shop)

Skagway's prominent people. He appeared law-abiding and always generous to a fault. He assisted many public enterprises and gave money to needy women and children. He even cared for stray pack dogs. By October, 1897, his well-established crime machine was in motion. Shell games along the White Pass Trail separated many a Klondiker from his money. Soapy, reigning as the uncrowned "King" of Skagway, commanded a band of more than three hundred thugs whom he called his "lambs." They turned in the proceeds from their crimes to Smith. He personally split the spoils among the hoodlums.

Soapy's share of the loot was always moderate and never questioned. He usually lost his entire share to his lieutenants in a faro game before the day was over. His true character was well known and was well illustrated by the legend about the time a zealous preacher came to Skagway.

The preacher, horrified at the town's wicked and sinful condition, proposed to do all he could to remedy the awful situation. The ambitious preacher consulted a wag who pointed out Soapy. The comic told the preacher to apply to the bearded gentleman for funds. Soapy Smith would come through with money for reform. Everyone regarded this as a huge joke on the innocent reformer.

However, Soapy received him warmly, told him his idea was a good one, and handed him $300 in cash. Encouraged by his success with Smith, the preacher started work in earnest. That night, Soapy's gang robbed him and took the original $300 — plus all of his other collections as a "profit" on their leader's "investment."

Soapy proclaimed for law and order, but reigned as the worst transgressor. He never overlooked a chance for illicit gold. His gang met all steamships in the guise of "special messengers." They lured the most prosperous passengers to haunts where they were relieved of their money. The gang erected tarpaper shacks on the Skagway docks and lured new arrivals with large signs, "Information Bureau," painted on the fronts of the structures. Unsuspecting

Klondikers seeking help would be questioned about finances and the "kindly" gentleman offering help would steer the victim to Jeff's Oyster Palace. There a rough-house fight would start between two "Lambs" and during the confusion the traveler's wallet would disappear.

Up and down the crowded passes Soapy's men were busy with the shell game or three card monte. Many innocents were deftly and suddenly parted from their funds. If any one dared raise a fuss, he found himself looking into the muzzle of a loaded Colt .45.

The Klondikers weren't the only ones to tangle with Soapy Smith's gang. The White Pass Railway also encountered the "Lambs." Camp No. 3, opened in early spring of 1898 with Mike Heney as construction chief, had a strict and simple rule:

"No liquor allowed in camp!"

Yet, a member of Soapy's gang established a gambling and drinking tent next to the railroad construction site. Mike Heney ordered Soapy's man away. The gang member refused to leave.

"I have as good a right to be here on the White Pass Trail as you and the railroad," he retorted.

The henchmen's contention was correct, but Heney was not one to worry over mere technical rights or legalities. Sending for Foy, the camp foreman, Heney pointed to a big rock just above the gambling den.

"Foy," he shouted in a loud voice, "that rock has to be out of there by 5 a.m. tomorrow morning and not a single minute later. Do you hear me?"

Early the next morning, Foy sent two members of the rock gang to plant dynamite beneath the boulder. They reported back to him at about ten minutes before 5 a.m. All was ready. At five until 5, Foy sent a man to the gambling tent to wake up the occupant. Replying in very bad language, Soapy's man refused to get up so early in the morning.

Foy went into the tent and stated flatly, "In one minute, by my watch, I will order the time fuse to be touched off on that dynamite. It will

This photograph shows Soapy Smith in a Skagway saloon on July 4, 1898, his day of triumph. A few days later he was dead. (Dedman's Photo Shop)

burn one more minute and then that rock will land directly on this tent."

Soapy's lieutenant replied angrily, "Foy, plain go to Hell."

Foy calmly replied, "I'm too busy this morning to go, but you will unless you jump lively. *Fire!*"

The crew outside lit the fuse and Foy used the sixty seconds allowed for the fuse to run and find shelter behind rock. The tent owner, wearing his long-handled underwear, quickly joined him.

Bang! went the dynamite. The rock crashed down. The avalanche completely destroyed the tent, liquor, and gambling equipment.

The foreman reported matter of factly to Big Mike, "The rock is down."

"What happened to Soapy's man?" queried Heney.

"The last that was seen of him," the foreman replied, "he was tearing down the trail towards Skagway in his long underwear, a cussin' and a fussin.'"

Why did the small community of Skagway permit an organization of highway robbers to make the town its headquarters? One thing that discouraged a clean-up campaign was that the crooks composed the largest gang ever to operate in North America. Few citizens had the courage to confront such a gang.

Skagway was an unorganized community and the entire police force was one U. S. deputy marshal — who happened to be on Soapy Smith's payroll.

There was a small U. S. Army detachment at Dyea which could be called in a major emergency. At the summit of White Pass, on the boundary between Alaska and Canada, were members of the Canadian Northwest Mounted Police. They maintained a strict supervision over their side of the border. But Soapy's gang wisely stayed out of Canada.

The thousands of travelers kept Skagway's good citizens so busy that the evil forces crept up on their blind side. Skagway's permanent residents seemed willing to accept the situation "if it just didn't get any worse."

Ironically, Soapy Smith's downfall was linked to developments revolving around the building of the White Pass and Yukon Route.

Samuel M. Graves, the president of the White Pass Railway, arrived in Skagway on July 2, 1898. He was invited to join with Soapy Smith in the honor of leading the 4th of July parade. Graves politely refused to be a part of the climax of Soapy's career.

On July 4th, Soapy led the parade, riding his gray horse. Following proudly were his "Lambs," all resplendent in new uniforms. The U. S. soldiers from Camp Dyea, brass bands, and Governor Brady of Alaska came next in the procession. The governor made a speech at the patriotic exercises and "Remember the Maine" was on every tongue.

On the Flag-draped rostrum in a place of honor next to the governor of Alaska sat the "King" of Skagway. This was Soapy Smith's great moment of triumph. The world was his oyster.

Four days later, Soapy Smith was dead.

The White Pass Railway's president, Samuel Graves, found his role bringing him into the conflict against Soapy Smith even though he only recently arrived in Skagway. Graves provided a vivid first-person account of the events that led to Soapy's downfall in his book *On the White Pass Payroll*, written just a few years after the incident.

Let's let Samuel Graves report what happened during that four days between Soapy Smith's triumph and downfall:

"Open violent robbery by 'Soapy's' gang was a daily occurence. They met all steamers arriving as regularly as the hotel touts and 'went through' any likely looking customers.

"Such was the state of affairs when I landed on July 2, 1898, and declined a courteous invitation from 'Soapy' to join him in riding through the streets at the head of the Fourth of July procession. Matters reached a climax when on July 6th 'Soapy's' men robbed a young man (J. D. Stewart) of approximately $3,000 in gold dust which he had just brought out over the White Pass from the Klondike. It was felt that whatever might be tolerated with regard to people 'Going in' the line must be drawn at robberies of gold coming out, if Skagway was to retain its boasted pre-eminence as the 'Gateway to the North!'"

"Skagway, July 8th, 1898—In times of peace prepare for war. 'There's two hundred cartridges anyway', said our purchasing agent, coming into the engineer's mess tent when we were at breakfast this morning and laying them down with four Winchester repeating rifles, one for each of use, on the breakfast table.

"It seems that the 'citizens' have determined to call Soapy to account and have notified him that the gold-dust must be returned within twenty-four hours, and that Soapy is not inclined to comply, saying that 'the money was lost in a square game.'

"The 'citizens' have called a mass meeting to consider what steps are to be taken. It looks like a fight and they look to us to lead them. After breakfast Heney, Hawkins and myself received an urgent invitation to attend a small, select meeting of 'prominent citizens' hastily summoned because of the feeling that nothing definite is likely to result from the mass meeting.

"Seventeen of us met and were called the 'merchants' committee,' but actually a vigilance committee, pure and simple, but no action was taken beyond electing a chairman and adjourning until 11 p.m., when it was agreed by all present that 'active measures are to be adopted!' Despite my protests I was unanimously chosen for chairman. However, I have, fortunately, our three engineers, Heney, Hislop, and Hawkins to advise me and it would be hard to duplicate such a trio.

"The first thing we decided was to send Heney and Hawkins up the Pass to prepare our camps for the hard fighting that seems inevitable, leaving Hislop and myself in Skagway to deal with the local situation and attend the meeting tonight. We are to keep in touch with one another by our private telephone, at the various camps.

"Having attended to these matters and our necessary daily grist of construction affairs, despite revolutions, I found an Italian bootblack and made a contract with him to black my boots for twenty-five cents (a shilling) which seems high unless you saw the boots.

"He had hardly got into action when I felt a touch on my shoulder and saw Hislop apparently deprecating the performance. 'This is hardly wise just now,' he said in gentle tones. I thought he meant that it was a poor investment as the boots would soon be as bad as ever. But he explained that public feeling was very excited and ran high, and while it did not nec-

essarily follow, of course, that a man was honest because he had dirty boots, on the other hand there was an irresistible presumption that if his boots were shining he must earn his living by questionable methods.

"The idea may be concisely formulated that 'the lustre of a man's character varies inversely with that of his boots!' I felt that my character was not sufficiently established to run any risks, and reluctantly cancelled the Italian's contract. But I had to pay him just the same. What did he care about my character?

"There are excited crowds all day in the streets, but Soapy's 'Lambs,' as he calls his 'volunteers' are working like London police, breaking up the groups. One almost expects to hear the familiar, 'Move on, now. Move on, please.'

"July 9th, The unexpected has happened. Soapy Smith is dead, and his lieutenants (including the United States Deputy Marshal)

Skagway citizens gather at the City Hall during a round-up of Soapy Smith's gang on July 9, 1898. (Provincial Archives of British Columbia)

are in irons, under guard of the 'merchants' committee' and hardly a shot fired. It is impossible to say which side was the most taken by surprise, but we recovered first and reaped an almost bloodless victory. It happened this way:

"The mass meeting was assembling at 9 o'clock on one of the wharfs, and two of their number had been detailed to hold the entrance and allow none of Soapy's friends in. No one was expecting any immediate fighting and there was only one revolver in the crowd, carried by a man named Reid, who was one of the two who had been appointed to hold the entrance.

"Our committee was not to meet until eleven, and no one expected any action until two or three in the morning. A ship had just arrived with 1,500 tons of rails and sleepers, for which we were in a hurry. She berthed at the adjoining wharf and Whiting, our Division Superintendent, and I had been down to see that they began unloading promptly.

"On our way back we had casually noticed the crowd assembling on the other wharf for the mass meeting, but neither of us paid any attention to it till we got off our wharf and were in the street leading to the wharf the crowd was on. We were about fifty yards from the two men who were holding the entrance, and the crowd was about seventy-five or eighty yards farther down the wharf when suddenly, Whiting said, 'By the Lord, here comes Soapy. Now look out.' 'Nonsense,' I said, 'he's only bluffing.'

"While I was speaking Soapy passed near enough to touch me. He was ostentatiously armed with a couple of big revolvers and a belt of cartridges, and carried a double-barrelled Winchester repeating rifle across his arm as he shouted to the crowd, 'Now chase yourselves home to bed.' I stood laughing till I saw he was followed about twenty-five yards behind, by a body-guard of fourteen of his picked men who were grimly silent and displayed no arms, though they were, notoriously, always armed to the teeth.

"These men followed Soapy past me and shut out my view. So I moved to the sidewalk

Workers were building the narrow gauge right-of-way on Tunnel Mountain in this 1898 photo. (H. Pollard Collection from Provincial Archives of Alberta)

and saw Soapy go up to Reid and make a bluff to hit him over the head with the barrel of his rifle. Reid put up one hand and protected his head by catching the barrel. Soapy, failing to shake off Reid's hold jerked back the rifle suddenly, which brought the muzzle against Reid's stomach. Reid, still holding Soapy's rifle with one hand, as before, put the other in his coat pocket and without taking it out, commenced to shoot his revolver. Soapy, at the same instant, began to pump shots from his Winchester into Reid's stomach. It would be impossible to say which fired first. The shots were absolutely simultaneous. Each fired four shots, though one of Reid's first shots had gone clean through Soapy's heart. It was not murder as much as spontaneous killing. Neither man had any intention of killing a moment before, but they must have seen death in each other's eyes at the last moment and both fired together.

A work train ascends a grade during construction of the narrow gauge near the White Pass summit in November, 1898. (Public Archives of Canada)

They fell together in a confused heap on the planking of the wharf, Soapy stone dead and Reid dying. It all happened in an instant.

"Meanwhile Soapy's body-guards were within twenty-five yards of the two prostrate men and the remaining entrance keeper, a little Irishman who worked for us.

"When Soapy's guards saw him fall they gave a furious yell and drew their 'guns,' as they called their heavy revolvers, and sprang forward for revenge on the unarmed crowd, and it looked as if what I had mistaken at first for a comedy was to be a shambles.

"But the little Irishman was the right man in the right spot and rose to the emergency. 'Be-gob, sorr,' he said to me an hour later, 'I had nawthin but a pincil when I saw them tigers makin' jumps for me.' But he had his quick wits and like a flash, he snatched Soapy's Winchester from the dead man's hands, and the leading 'tiger' saw Murphy's eye gazing at him along the sights.

"Involuntarily, the 'tiger' checked his rush, and was passed by another of Soapy's guards. That instant Murphy shifted and covered the new leader and the same thing happened. By the time Murphy had covered the third leader, the 'tigers' behind realized that some of them

were sure to be shot and somehow they were not in such a hurry.

"The men in front, realizing that they were not being supported, looked around to see why. The rush was over and in another instant the whole fourteen broke and fled.

"At that moment the crowd on the wharf, who had stood paralyzed with terror, became a blood-thirsty pack of wolves and with a yell, they started in pursuit, unarmed. They swept past us and in another moment the crowd, jumping over the dead Soapy and the dying Reid, tore past us yelling, 'Get your guns, citizens.'

"When they had gone by I ran over to our office tent and phoned Heney at Camp Three and Hawkins at Camp Five what had happened and arranged with them to hold the Pass and let no one go by without an order signed by Hyslop or me, and to hold their men ready to come down and help us clear up the town if we called for help. But it wasn't necessary.

"We put armed guards on all the wharfs, with orders to shoot on sight if anyone tried to escape in a boat. Their escape by land or water was cut off and we proceeded to round up the gang. Some tried to get away in boats and were caught by our guards. Some tried the Pass and

Heney and Hawkins got them, and the rest we got by an organized search of the town before they had time to rally, except a few who took to the mountains, but we will starve them out.

"We captured more than we could find jail room for, so we selected thirty-one of the leaders and let the rest go, to get out of town and keep out. Now, our problem is to save the men we have in jail from the infuriated mob, who are clamouring for their blood.

"July 11th. We have got the men who escaped to the mountains, including three of Soapy's head men. But Reid's death has made the feeling very bitter and we are at our wits' end to guard the prisoners from the fury of the mob. We have no jail to keep them in — nothing but a board shanty where they have hardly standing room and huddle together like sheep, while the mob, night and day, howl around the shanty for their blood. We have detailed some of the railwaymen, whom we can trust, to guard the shanty.

"Meanwhile, the committee is taking evidence of the prisoners, one by one, partly in the hope of implicating some of the merchants and 'hotel' keepers, who are suspected of having dealings with Soapy, chiefly to give the mob time to quiet down. We tell them that if they hang any of the prisoners, they will close their mouths effectively, and frustrate our efforts to get the men we need the most. Up to this date this has been effective in preventing bloodshed, but the mob is getting impatient.

"Two men of our committee are opposed to our policy of holding the prisoners in terror, and examining them, and they advocate turning the whole bunch loose and letting the mob do what they please.

"We suspect these men of being themselves implicated and their idea is that if the prisoners were released, the mob would either hang the ones who know anything, or if not, there would no longer be any compulsion for them to give evidence. In either case their mouths would be closed which seems to be what these two Committeemen want.

"July 13th. The mob is now gradually quieting down and now there is no danger of blood-

shed. The prisoners have disclosed nothing of value to us and, encouraged, we think, by their friends on the Committee, are beginning to talk about their 'rights.' They could give us a good deal of trouble if they dared us, of course, we have no shadow of law to warrant holding them, and still less for taking the money from them, and using it to pay for the stolen gold dust, and for a fund to pay for legal prosecution of those against whom we have evidence, and also to pay for the cost of deporting the others.

"This being so, before the mob got too tame, I took one of the prisoners who was asserting his 'rights,' by the shoulder and led him to the window of our room, where he could look down on the mob, and said to him, 'You are quite

A locomotive rolls near Inspiration Point, by the trail to White Pass summit, in this 1899 photo. (H. Pollard Collection from Provincial Archives of Alberta)

right. We have no authority for holding you a moment against your will. If you say the word I will turn you loose into that mob this minute. What do you say?'

"This was more than he expected, so he began to hedge, as I had hoped. Then I said, 'If you don't want us to turn you loose this minute, you must sign this paper,' and I drew up a written request to the committee, to hold and protect him until he could be handed over to lawful authorities and, in consideration of our doing this, authority for us to apply all the money found on him for the uses of the Committee. He demurred at signing and wanted to consult the other prisoners but I said, 'No. Sign or step outside. We can't be bothered with you any longer.' Then he signed and we put him in another room and sent for all the prisoners, one at a time, and repeated the same proceedings, until all had signed, before we allowed them to confer with one another.

"This got us not only out of a false position, but provided funds (1) to pay for the stolen gold-dust, (2) to carry on the prosecution of the six or seven (including the United States marshal) against whom we had legal evidence, and (3) to deport those whom we cannot prosecute.

"The first batch, fourteen of the latter, go south on the 'Athenian' tomorrow, and I am going on the same ship, as the work of the Committee is now completed anyhow, and I have to go to Victoria to see the Provincial Government, to let us work beyond the Summit, as the Dominion Government has, high-handedly, refused to let us work there, in spite of the fact that the ground is within the province of British Columbia. They can only delay us, as we have a Dominion as well as a Provincial charter.

"I may say that the men we sent to trial were all convicted, and given heavy sentences, including the United States marshal. The deported men who went on the 'Athenian' with me had the bad luck, on landing in Seattle, to run into the very arms of the Chief of Police who was waiting at the gang-plank to meet his sister-in-law. He recognized some of them and

took the lot on suspicion."

Later, in a report, Mr. Graves said:

"It turned out that most of them were 'wanted' in various places in the United States, and several were hanged and others given long terms in prison for their various crimes. So ended the episode of the killing of Soapy Smith.

"After the events above described, the want of some more orthodox body than a vigilante committee was felt and the citizens decided to hold an election which was done without a vestige of legal warrant, and a Mayor and City Council elected and a Chief of Police (or Deputy Marshal) appointed and, in short, a complete municipal organization was perfected. This body granted franchises (The White Pass got one for our Broadway Street track) and this City government was carried on for a year or two, until Congress passed a law providing for municipal elections in Alaska.

"The reaction from Soapy Smith's regime was so complete that not one of the acts or transactions of this unique body was ever questioned, and the first legal municipal council elected in Skagway ratified and adopted them *en bloc.*"

Frank Reid — the ex-school teacher and Indian fighter who became Skagway's town surveyor — was buried in the Skagway cemetery. The funeral contained the largest group of mourners ever to assemble in Alaska. On his Alaska granite tombstone is the statement in bold letters: "He Gave His Life For the Honor of Skagway."

Many pioneer residents of Skagway believed another version of the dual killing. This account contends that instead of being killed by Frank Reid, Soapy was shot by a bystander. This version of the incident holds that the person who fired the shot was perhaps an employee of the White Pass Railway. Those who believe this story say that the person fired while Soapy and Reid struggled over the Winchester. The old-timers who tell the account maintain that the bullet removed from Soapy Smith would not fit Reid's gun. They also contend that the bullet passed from Soapy's left side to his right. Since he and Reid were facing each

FIRST EXCURSION TRAIN IN ALASKA
SKAGWAY, JULY 21, 1898

Travelers pose happily in Skagway aboard flatcars pulled by the White Pass and Yukon line's first engine, a Brooks 2-6-0, during the railway's initial excursion. The date was July 21, 1898. (Dedman's Photo Shop)

other, Reid could not have fired the shot, they claim.

Most people who saw the shooting agreed with President Graves' account of how Reid killed Soapy Smith.

One thing was certain: Soapy Smith was dead. Skagway was no longer a town of sin and vice controlled by that uncrowned "King" of Skagway.

The same day that Frank Reid died brought the arrival of Alaska's first locomotive. A second-hand Brooks 2-6-0, the locomotive was barged up from Seattle and unloaded at the Skagway docks. The very next day the engine chuffed and puffed for four miles out of town, pulling a flat car or two loaded with thrilled townspeople. This was the first train to run in Alaska and the furthest north any train had operated on the North American continent.

The construction of the White Pass and Yukon Railway through the rugged terrain and in freezing temperatures took two years for completion. The labor turnover resulted in approximately 35,000 men working on the project. The cost of the railroad was slightly more than

$12 million, or well over $100,000 a mile. The narrow gauge's cost, therefore, was substantially more on a per mile basis than most standard gauge railroads built during the same era. The price tag for building the White Pass would have been even more if its backers had decided on the wider gauge.

While many railroads crossed sections of difficult terrain, almost every mile of the White Pass and Yukon route was rugged. The railway's *average* grade was 2.6 per cent, as compared with a *maximum* of only 1 per cent for the Western Pacific, built a few years later over the rugged Sierra Nevada of California. The steepest portion of the White Pass line was a 3.9 per cent grade carved from solid rock in the mountains. This part of the route was constructed only after workers were dangled on ropes down the mountain sides so that they could drill holes for blasting powder.

Big Mike Heney took good care of his men and few required hospitaliation in Skagway. Most of those requiring hospitalization were treated for severe frost bite or injured fingers or toes.

The White Pass remained in troubled waters — not because of vice, crime, or politics, but by virtue of nature herself. The construction of the White Pass Railway presented the most difficult project ever engineered at the time. It was more than a thousand miles from the base of supplies in Seattle to Skagway. Communications between the two ports were confined to letters carried by the coastal steamships, which operated on very uncertain schedules.

They therefore retained Brydon-Jack, an English-trained engineer, to watch over the work and see that it progressed in accordance with the contract. The North Americans had preconceived ideas of European railway engineers and were apprehensive about the newcomer. They worried and asked themselves, "Would he become a problem and be difficult about the construction?"

Their concern over Brydon-Jack proved unfounded. He was young and fit, and willing to

These proud citizens posed for this picture at Log Cabin on July 6, 1899, during the White Pass' first trip to Bennett from Skagway. Flatcars carried seats for the trip. (Provincial Archives of British Columbia)

Heavy duty construction equipment simply wasn't available in Skagway. Despite this handicap, Mike Heney and his men worked with horses, shovels, and black powder, carving the right-of-way along a wall of solid rock. The British capitalists did not trust or feel at ease with the skills of Canadian and American engineers.

meet the hazards of the climate and the rough conditions in the construction camps. Before long, Mike Heney, along with John Hislop, the chief surveyor, and E. C. Hawkins, the chief engineer, were proud to work with Brydon-Jack. They were fond of him and admired his fellowship and pluck.

The young supervisor was not toughened, however, to the rigorous sub-zero weather that ruled the mountains a few miles north of Skagway. The hard climbing, rough life, and constant exposure to cold soon brought him down with pneumonia. The Americans rushed him back to the hospital at Skagway, where he died the next day. All the members of the staff felt the loss of their new friend and his courage and honesty. E. C. Hawkins, the American engineer, was appointed in Brydon-Jack's place as supervisor for the British capitalists paying the bills.

The first construction gangs represented men from all walks of life. Most of them started out to reach the Klondike gold fields, but went broke. They still wanted to head north as soon as possible. They continually came and went. The maximum number employed at any one time was a little more than 2,000. At other times the labor force fell to 700. Their need for money and the cold weather stimulated the men to work hard. But climatic conditions, the difficult terrain, and the remoteness of the base of supplies combined to slow the work.

Construction of the right-of-way required vast quantities of tricky black powder. At Rocky Point, a cliff 120 feet in height, 70 feet in depth, and 20 feet in thickness was blasted away.

The fact that the railroad was narrow gauge made the construction easier than if the project had been standard gauge. The broader right-of-way would have required even more work. A 250-foot tunnel penetrated in solid granite. No tunnel in the world was built with greater difficulty. The only tunnel on the White Pass, it went through a perpendicular barrier of rock which jutted out of the mountainside like a giant buttress. Men had to carry all the machinery and equipment up the steep cliffs. The workers clung to only the barest of footholds on the granite barricade. Some worked from rope slings as they drilled the first holes. A wood trestle over Glacier Gorge led to the tunnel's south portal. A narrow ledge blasted from solid granite served as the north portal.

In the 20.4 mile battle to the summit, a steel

The wagon road and subsequently the narrow-gauge right-of-way were carved on the rugged mountains. This 1899 photo was made near Rocky Point. (H. Pollard Collection from Provincial Archives of Alberta)

cantilever bridge spectacularly spanned a deep, narrow canyon. The rushing creek bed was 215 feet below the bridge, which required until 1901 for completion. Before it was finished, a tortuous switchback was necessary to get around the gulch.

Below this bridge in Dead Horse Gulch, the White Pass Trail winds its way, worn into the native rock by the thousands of sourdoughs and Klondikers who formed the long black line of half-crazed gold seekers.

From sea level at Skagway the three-foot narrow gauge railroad winds its cliff-hanging way to the summit of White Pass. In twenty-one miles it climbs 2,885 feet. The highest point on the line is Milepost 33: Log Cabin, British Columbia, with an altitude of 2,916 feet.

When completed, the White Pass and Yukon Railway stretched 110.7 miles from terminal to terminal. Of this total, 20.4 miles are in Alaska,

This photograph, taken in June, 1898, shows workmen laying track down Broadway in Skagway as the narrow gauge led from the harbor to the rugged mountains so difficult for travelers. (Cy Martin Collection)

32.2 miles are in British Columbia, and 58.1 miles are in the Yukon Territory.

The fact that the line crossed portions of three political divisions — the then Territory of Alaska, the Province of British Columbia, and the Yukon Territory — created complications that resulted in the formation of three companies to operate the route.

The companies formed as part of the White Pass and Yukon Route were the Pacific and Arctic Railway and Navigation Co., operating in Alaska; the British Columbia Yukon Railway, serving the portion in British Columbia, and the British Yukon Railway, operating in the Yukon Territory.

The White Pass and Yukon Railway Co., Ltd., a Canadian corporation, owned the three companies that held the rights to operate the route from Skagway to Whitehorse.

Blasting and hacking their way over rugged terrain, construction crews pushed the tracks to the summit of White Pass on February 20, 1899. The workmen were laying track along the headwaters of Lake Bennett in early July. While laborers made the assault through White Pass, other construction crews began working from Whitehorse. Their goal was to build through Carcross (Caribou Crossing) and meet the workmen that began in Skagway.

Even though the line was not completed, freight and passenger service linked Skagway and Whitehorse after the tracks reached the White Pass summit. Horse-drawn wagons and sleds provided the means of travel over the area not covered by tracks.

Construction continued, but rumors as well as the rugged mountains slowed laying of the tracks.

Above, Locomotive 3, returning the first passenger train from White Pass summit on February 20, 1899, is silhouetted against snow in this photo by pioneer photographer E. A. Hegg. (Public Archives of Canada)

Below, the first through train over the White Pass and Yukon route to Bennett heads south to Skagway after reaching the summit of White Pass on July 6, 1899. (Provincial Archives of British Columbia)

First through train enroute to Bennett

The first passenger train to White Pass summit crosses a bridge before entering the tunnel on February 20, 1899. (Provincial Archives of British Columbia)

When a gold strike was reported along the Fan Tail Trail near Lake Atlin in British Columbia during the late summer of 1898, more than 1,500 laborers promptly stopped work and left for the area to seek their fortunes. The exit of the workers was not the only loss that faced the railroad: White Pass records showed that the line's picks and shovels, useful for digging gold as well as right-of-ways, went with the men.

Despite problems with workers and the terrain, construction of the White Pass continued. Laborers began grading the right-of-way along the shore of Lake Bennett in early summer, 1898. The railway's line skirted the lake for twenty-seven miles along a crooked but level route. The major problem presented for construction in this area pertained to the climate: some ground was frozen (permafrost) to bed rock, making it difficult to build the right-of-way. The fact that the lake could be navigated during the summer sped construction. Steamers carried men and material to camps at various points around the lake.

After the ordeals of rugged terrain and freezing weather, the southbound construction gang met its northbound counterpart at Carcross. The joyful day was July 29, 1900.

"Golden Spike" completion ceremonies had become almost traditional for railroads, big or small, since the famous "last spike" ritual linked America's first transcontinental line at Promontory Point, Utah, in 1869. The White Pass "Golden Spike" ceremony was held at Carcross. Attending were the railroad's president, Samuel Graves, and a colorful group of Canadian and American dignitaries, both civilian and military.

Before the last spike was driven, the first regular passenger train arrived from Skagway and was waiting on a siding until it could go on north. An eastern professor of geology got off the train and began to examine the newly blasted rock. After chipping a few rock samples from the cut, he rushed over to an Irish section hand who was tamping the ballast. The excited professor said, "My man, do you know that broken stone you are using for ballasting the track is a highly mineralized paleozoic formation, and probably worth not less than $10 a ton?"

The Irishman lit his pipe leisurely. Taking a few puffs, he replied, "Well, I want ye to understand that the bist is noen too good for the White Pass."

The actual ceremony began after an experienced track man started the golden spike. The event was a highly entertaining affair.

"The spike stood upright and gleaming beside the rail," the railroad's president later recalled. "The officials who were to share the honor of driving the spike home approached it with considerable misgiving, as it was generally conceded by both the crowd and the officials that enthusiasm for the task might not completely overcome the effects of the Yukon's lavish liquid hospitality."

Mr. Graves, being a good host, invited the senior American Army officer to "strike the first blow." After a series of disastrous attempts, the spike, while bent, was clearly the winner.

Others took up the challenge, cheered on by the celebrating crowd. But the spike by now had the general characteristics of a piece of boiled spaghetti. Still it successfully stood its ground. The official party eyed the spike in si-

Above, this gathering celebrated the completion of the narrow gauge to Lake Bennett on July 6, 1899. The W. P. & Y. train arrived from Skagway. (H. Pollard Collection from the Provincial Archives of Alberta)

Below, this crowd gathers for the Golden Spike ceremony held July 29, 1900, at Carcross, Yukon Territory, to celebrate laying of the White Pass' last rails. (Provincial Archives of British Columbia)

After battling snow and steep grades, the first passenger train reached the summit of White Pass on February 20, 1899. This photograph recorded that triumphant occasion. (Provincial Archives of British Columbia)

lence, and finally accepting defeat, slowly retired from the affray to partake of better things.

On leaving the scene, Mr. Graves caught the eye of the track superintendent, and it was he who replaced the historic spike with a less noble one. Then he unceremoniously drove it home with a few well directed blows of his sledge.

A bronze plaque on a stone cairn near the Carcross station commemorates the momentous ceremony for driving the White Pass and Yukon Route golden spike. The plaque was dedicated July 29, 1965, during a sober ceremony marking the sixty-fifth anniversary of the line's completion. Attending were Roy Minter, assistant to the president of the White Pass, and other leaders. The plaque reads:

THE GOLDEN SPIKE

Construction of the White Pass & Yukon Railway began on May 27, 1898 at Skagway, Alaska, during the height of the great Klondike Gold Rush.

Undaunted by those who said the railway could not be built, a small group of devoted White Passers composed of Contractor Michael J. Heney; Chief Engineer, "E. C." Hawkins; Assistant Chief Engineer, John Hislop, and the railway's first President, Samuel H. Graves, pushed the work to completion. After overcoming almost insurmountable construction problems, the last rail was laid at this spot on July 29, 1900. On that day "The Golden Spike" was set in place and with a cheering boisterous crowd of Alaskan and Yukoners in attendance, Samuel H. Graves drove it home. The job was done.

To the thousands of men who gave their strength and talent to the construction of the White Pass and Yukon Railway, this plaque is respectfully dedicated on the 65th anniversary of the White Pass & Yukon Route's "Golden Spike."

This narrow gauge passenger train paused by a water tank on the shore of Lake Bennett in Summer, 1900. (Provincial Archives of British Columbia)

Fifty Years of Railroading

CHAPTER III

The booming Klondike traffic overwhelmed the White Pass and Yukon Route with cargo. The line's little three-foot gauge locomotives busily pulled coaches and freight cars over the route that previously had been so difficult to travel. To serve its traffic efficiently, the railway added to its motive power during the years and retired equipment that no longer was useful. (*See appendix for roster of equipment.*)

The White Pass and Yukon purchased five engines in 1898 from the Columbia and Puget Sound Railway when that line converted to standard gauge. These locomotives represented an odd assortment of power. The acquisitions included two ex-Utah and Northern Brooks Moguls (No. 1 and No. 2), Grant (No. 3) and Baldwin (No. 5) 2-8-0's, and a small Baldwin (No. 4) eight-wheeler.

Since all of these locomotives were fifteen to twenty years old and left much to be desired,

the company decided to acquire better equipment.

In January, 1899, two first-class engines were shipped north by barge to Skagway. These 2-8-0's (No. 6 and No. 7) were brand new Baldwin Vauclain Compounds with a tractive effort of 21,000 pounds. A third engine built in 1897 was purchased and shipped for construction duties. It was a three-truck Climax (No. 8) from the Pacific Contract Co.

After the completion of the railway to Whitehorse, river steamers could operate straight through to Dawson City and beyond without any portages or dangerous rapids. A traveler or cargo could go from Skagway to St. Michael, on the Bering Sea, in relative comfort by rail and river steamer. With the continuation of the gold rush boom in the north, the White Pass needed more locomotives. Two used Moguls were purchased in the spring of 1900. One of unknown manufacture came from the Columbia and Western (No. 64) and the other, a used Brooks Mogul (No. 63), was purchased from an unknown source. They arrived at Skagway in June, 1900.

The railroad also purchased a used Brooks Mogul (No. 65) from the Columbia and Western early in the spring of 1900. These were accompanied by four brand new Baldwins, and consisted of three 10-wheelers (No. 59, No. 60, and No. 62) and a 2-8-0 (No. 61). These 10-wheelers were very successful and two more (No. 66 and 67) were purchased direct from Baldwin in 1901.

However, the Vauclain compounds (renumbered No. 56 and No. 57 in 1900) were not too successful. One (No. 57) was sold in 1906 and the other (No. 56) simplified in 1907.

Even with the early power, the completion of the railroad to Whitehorse dropped the freight rate of 12 cents a pound to 2 cents a pound. Six months after the White Pass began regular train service in 1900, the Klondike boom was over. Using the narrow gauge railway to import heavy machinery from the manufacturing centers to the south, the mining companies quickly worked out the gold bearing gravel.

The City of Dawson entered a new phase of civic development and proudly announced it was the metropolis of the North. But clearer heads saw the signs of decline. The pick and the gold pan grew less important. Giant dredges came to claw the gold-bearing gravels from the creeks beds. The need for manpower dwindled and the Yukon's population began to drift away. The prospectors either went home or to the fresh gold rush at Nome, Alaska. For a single season the White Pass narrow gauge prospered. Then traffic fell off and the company diversified into the Yukon River steamboat business. It constructed a number of paddle-wheel steamers to ply on the river between Whitehorse and Dawson City.

The White Pass ran its own stern-wheelers because river service was irregular and unreliable. The British Yukon Navigation Company was organized to operate the river service and became the River Division of the White Pass and Yukon Route. The division's steamers ran for more than a half century. Trucks replaced the last steamer in the summer of 1955.

The voyage downstream from Whitehorse to Dawson City aboard one of the stern-wheelers

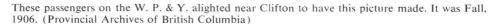

These passengers on the W. P. & Y. alighted near Clifton to have this picture made. It was Fall, 1906. (Provincial Archives of British Columbia)

averaged three days. Upstream from Dawson to the railhead at Whitehorse took five to six days. Three of the boats remained on the river bank at Whitehorse in June, 1966, as reminders of the days when the British Yukon Navigation Company operated a fleet of majestic vessels from railhead to docks at Dawson City.

The sternwheelers *Whitehorse, Casca,* and *Klondike* were the last steamers to regularly ply the mighty Yukon. The *Whitehorse* was built in 1901 and rebuilt in 1930. Despite her 1,120 tons, she drew only three feet three inches of water. This shallow draft, coupled with a flat bottom, was necessary for operations on the Dawson City to Whitehorse run.

The sand bar at the entrance to Lake Lebarge always created a serious hazard. The channel, narrow and shallow, became virtually impassable after a long dry spell. The river boat captains were required to "walk" their ladies across the bar on her huge stern paddle wheel.

The stern-wheeler would back into the channel so the paddlewheel could pull, instead of push, the boat along. The mate stationed aft with a sounding pole while the craft splashed slowly backward. The hull bumped, quivered, and jarred along the silt bottom. The paddle blades churned up more mud than water. For twenty minutes the issue would remain in doubt. Then, with some luck, the mate would call out "deep water."

The paddle steamer was over the bar and in safe water again.

Dangerous waters loomed again at Five Finger Rapids. Between Carmack's and Fort Selkirk, the Yukon is nearly blocked by a broken and ragged wall of rock. The mighty river rushes through five narrow gaps in the barrier. During the gold rush, many a prospector met his doom when homemade raft or boat slammed against the rocks. Only the most skillful pilots dared take a steamer through Five Fingers on the swift current.

The run was so risky that it was never attempted when the wind was blowing. The boat raced through the rapids in two minutes. One captain of the retired fleet mused: "If a pilot missed the channel the first time, he didn't get

Typical of early day White Pass shipments, this gold rests in the Skagway depot on arrival from the Klondike. (Provincial Archives of British Columbia)

another chance."

Churning upstream, the stern-wheelers again faced the swift current at the "Fingers." The pilots "winched" their boats through the narrow rapids. A cable was anchored from the port side to the rocky shore and to the forward deck winch. Winding in the cable pulled the river boat slowly upstream.

Even the efficient narrow gauge had problems. This wreck occurred just south of the tunnel in Summer, 1900. (Provincial Archives of British Columbia)

These Yukon river boats took a vacation when cold weather hit and tied up in Whitehorse for Winter, 1904. (Provincial Archives of British Columbia)

The Yukon river boat Casca III, operated by White Pass system, performs freight duty in the early 1950's before end of this service. (Dedman's Photo Shop)

All of the paddle-wheelers were wood burners in the early days, but between 1945 and 1955 they were converted to burn oil.

This ended an era for many residents who made a living cutting wood for the boats each winter. They stacked it a frequent intervals along the banks. In the summer, they helped load the wood aboard when needed. Some boats burned a cord an hour while under a full head of steam.

The *Whitehorse,* oldest steamer on the beach, was known to the river men as "The Old Gray Mare." The first *Casca* was dismantled in 1911 and the second was wrecked on July 9, 1936, at Rink Rapids on the Yukon. She was a total loss except for the engines and other machinery. *Casca III,* 1,300 tons, the White Pass River Division flagship, was built at Whitehorse in 1937 by the British Yukon Navigation Company.

The original *Klondike* sank and a new sternwheeler was built in 1936, using the machinery and boiler from the wreck. The boiler came from another old steamer, the S. S. *Yukoner,* which was retired at Whitehorse in the early 1900's.

The *Klondike,* launched in June, 1937, was 210 feet long, with a forty-four foot beam. For years this large freighter carried ore concentrates from the Mayo silver-lead mines. In 1945, extra staterooms were added for passenger accommodation. In 1953, a bar and lounge were provided and special riverboat tours were organized. Unusually low water on the river forced cancellations of several tours. Other problems forced the *Klondike* to join her sister on the beach in the summer of 1955.

The Canadian Government preserved the *Klondike* as a National Historic Site in 1966. The White Pass and Yukon Railway presented this vessel, along with the *Casca* and the *Whitehorse,* after the company's River Division became inoperative.

A National Historic Site at Dawson City preserved the S. S. *Keno* in 1964. The White Pass also donated this vessel to the government.

The S. S. *Tutshi* operated as a tourist steamer from the train stop at Carcross to Ben-my-

The White Pass tourist steamer Tutshi, which once met the narrow gauge at Carcross, was retired and displayed there. (Cy Martin Photograph)

Chree. Thousands of passengers who came by train from Skagway made the trip. The paddle-wheeler leisurely took them through the beautiful inland lakeway to the fabulous garden spot for a close look at the towering glaciers. Change of schedules by the coastal steamers eliminated the chance for a stopover at Carcross. This promptly beached the little *Tutshi,* whose Indian name means "deep dark water."

Piloting the Yukon steamers called for great skill and a genius for "reading water." The breaks in the surface and the coloring told the depth and nature of the channel as it changed from day to day. The skillful river pilot was replaced by the modern and equally skillful tractor-trailer driver on the Highway Division of the White Pass Route.

In March, 1901, the company bought the winter stage line of the Canadian Development Company, operating horse-drawn vehicles from Whitehorse to Dawson City. This operation earned the name "The Royal Mail Service," since it carried the mail during the closed sea-

Railroaders posed proudly on June 7, 1900, when the first W. P. & Y. trains rolled over the line into Whitehorse. (Dedman's Photo Shop)

son on the river. The horse-drawn vehicles remained in regular service during the winter months until 1921.

While the river remained open in 1901, the White Pass built roadhouses at intervals along the trail and stored supplies for men and horses. When the snow and ice hit in the fall of 1902, the service was fully equipped with horses, sleighs, and supplies.

The winter route between Whitehorse and Dawson, locally called "The Overland Trail," portaged across two river bends and shortened the distance between terminals to three hundred and thirty miles, or seventy miles less than the river route.

On November 2, 1902, the first stage left Whitehorse with two passengers. They were Herbert Wheeler, the newly appointed superintendent of the stage service (later president of the White Pass and Yukon Railway) and George A. Jeckell, a school teacher who later became comptroller of the Yukon Territory.

A regular weekly service was established and maintained regardless of the severe weather. A minimum of two hundred horses was required to operate the mail, express, and passenger stages. Four-wheel stages ran during the periods from early freeze-up until the ice was solid and there was sufficient snow for sleds. Roadhouses and stables stood approximately twenty miles apart. Food for the riders and fodder for the horses were stored at each stop.

The roadhouses were small hotels of logs,

The W. P. & Y. used this advertisement in 1946 to tell people about the picturesque narrow gauge rides.

heated by roaring wood fires. They provided comfortable beds and good meals. Moose, caribou, and mountain sheep steaks and roasts were frequently served. Meals were $1.50, while beds cost $1 per night. Baggage up to twenty-five pounds for each passenger was carried free in the "boot" of the stages. Passenger fares were $125 one way, plus roadhouse expenses.

During the deep winter months, sleighs drawn by four to six horse teams carried fourteen passengers, mail, baggage, and express. Charcoal burning foot warmers were changed at each road house. Buffalo robes were supplied for the passengers. In spring and fall, the drivers fought floods, washouts, and mud and slides, — not to speak of the ordeals of coping with several river crossings on slush ice.

At Whitehorse, there was a horse hospital operated by a veterinarian. The company maintained complete carriage and sleigh, harness, and blacksmith shops. Stages were built from the ground up, harness made and repaired, and the seats upholstered.

The stage "skinners" wore coon-skin coats and had long red sashes tied around their waists, like the coureuer-de-bois of early French Canada. They also wore soft fur-backed leather gloves with silk, or woolen liners. On extremely cold days they held the reins in one hand, while beating the other against a shoulder to keep it from freezing. The seat of honor, reserved for favored passengers especially in good weather, was up on the high front seat beside the driver.

A typical cold day in front of the Whitehorse depot found the passengers bundled to their eyes as the driver climbed up to his perch and cracked his whip. The horses were off at a sharp trot down Front Street, starting the 330 mile journey which would land the stage in Dawson City on the fifth or sixth day. Depending on weather and trail conditions, the stage reached three or four posts each day. The regular schedule called for a five-day trip, but in an emergency the run could be made in three days.

The drivers came from a hearty breed of men who could battle even the most severe weather. When travel began to decline during the last years of the stages, drivers did not leave a post if the temperature fell to lower than forty degrees below zero.

After the gold fever subsided, the narrow gauge White Pass caught its breath and shook out the engine roster. The two original Brooks Moguls (No. 1 and No. 2) were rebuilt in 1900 and renumbered No. 51 and No. 52. The Grant, 2-8-0 (No. 3) received a straight stack, extended smoke box, new cylinders, and was renumbered 53. Most of the other engines were sold during the next few years.

The Tanana Mines Railway, near Fairbanks, bought the Baldwin 4-4-0 (No. 4) in 1905. The short Klondike Mines Railway at Dawson City purchased three engines: a Brooks 2-6-0 (No. 63) in 1902, a Baldwin 2-8-0 (No. 5) in 1904, and a Baldwin 2-8-0, Vauclain compound (No. 57) in 1906. The Climax (No. 8) was sold to the Maytown Lumber Company in 1903.

The railroad ordered new locomotives from Baldwin in 1907 (No. 68) and in 1908 (No.

A 1901 storm piled snow high around this narrow gauge train on Broadway, in downtown Skagway. Weather seldom stopped trains. (Dedman's Photo Shop)

69). These were large 2-8-0's with 24,000 pounds of tractive effort.

In 1910 the White Pass constructed a ten and a quarter mile branch line to a large copper mine.

The company paid regular dividends throughout this period. Until the start of World War I, the railway could count on moving 10,000 to 16,000 passengers a year, and expect to carry 30,000 tons of freight annually.

The railroad's business began to decline at the beginning of World War I, when Dawson and the Klondike started to feel an economic pinch. Falling gold production and the demands of the war were changing the old pattern of northern life. A great era was passing. Dawson City and the Yukon would never be quite the same.

At the start of World War I, gold mining slackened and there wasn't enough lead, zinc, or silver mined to compensate for the loss. The tourist industry, which might have helped, was virtually non-existent. Dividends declined on the railroad and ceased altogether in 1914. A complete financial reorganization of the company was necessary in 1918. After that, operations continued mainly through the sheer determination of the management and very little else.

Despite the decline, the White Pass and Yukon refused to quit. With dogged determination it ran its trains whenever there was freight to haul. The population of Whitehorse dropped to less than four hundred, and Dawson City's population was approximately a thousand. The notion that the Yukon was finished never occurred to the optimistic Yukoners who were sticking it out. With an uncertain future for both the Yukon and itself, the White Pass and Yukon Route entered into the Roaring Twenties — with little to roar about.

Throughout the Twenties, the mining activities in the Klondike and Mayo districts kept the wheels turning slowly and the Yukon refused to die. Additional income for the Terri-

During the early 1930's the great depression struck the Yukon, just as it hit other sections of the world. Both tourist travel and the volume of freight dropped to a trickle. Despite the economic situation, however, the whistle of the steam locomotive served as a reminder that Canada's most northerly railroad was not quitting. The line's management, perhaps hearing a faint military drum beat in the background, believed the railroad would be needed in the future. Its officials strived for the White Pass and Yukon to survive the Thirties.

The railway moved approximately 12,000

Snow remained only in the mountains when this train rolled down Broadway during late Spring in the 1920's. (Dedman's Photo Shop)

tory's dwindling economy came from the tourists who travelled North each summer to visit the land of the midnight sun. They came to Skagway by ship and rode the train over the St. Elias Mountains to Whitehorse. Here they boarded the Yukon riverboats for a leisurely trip down stream or north to Dawson City.

The White Pass almost joined the ghost railways of the world. Not a single new engine was added to the roster from 1908 to 1938.

tons of freight annually from 1931 to 1935. This volume compared with the approximately 30,000 tons of freight carried each year prior to World War I.

Seeking new revenues, the White Pass in the spring of 1937 organized an air service to carry mail, freight, express, and passengers throughout the Yukon Territory. This air line was sold, however, in December, 1941, to Yukon Southern Air Transport.

The discovery of silver, lead, and zinc in the Mayo mining district brought ore shipments to Skagway via the White Pass river and rail divisions. Even so, everything came to a virtual standstill during the winter.

The approach of World War II stirred the Yukon's economy to some extent. This activity created enough business to save the White Pass for its effort during the conflict.

The locomotive roster dwindled to only eight operating engines. One of the line's original locomotives, No. 56, was replaced in 1938 with a new Baldwin 2-8-2, No. 70, an inside-frame "Mike" that could be contrasted to the Denver Rio Grande's narrow gauge "Mikes" with outside frames. An immediate success, No. 70 was called the "best narrow-gauge steam engine ever built." A sister engine, No. 71, arrived in 1939. The company returned to the used locomotive market in 1940 and found a pair of Alco 2-8-2's (No. 80 and No. 81) on the Sumpter Valley Railroad.

On December 7, 1941, Pearl Harbor burst upon the scene with unprecedented impact. All too quickly the hidden fears of the Alaskans and Yukoners became a horrible reality. The Northwest lay naked and vulnerable to the Japanese.

Governmental officials early in 1941 recommended an overland link between the continental United States and Alaska, but the public received the proposal without enthusiasm. The objections disappeared after Pearl Harbor. The United States Army had one hundred fighter planes in Alaska. A long and highly exposed sea route spliced the United States with Fairbanks and Anchorage. If the Japanese won a foothold on this vital route, they could choke delivery of Allied war supplies.

The only answer was a 1,522-mile all-weather highway from British Columbia to Fairbanks. This artery connected the northern terminal of standard gauge rail in Canada with the terminal of the government-owned Alaska Railroad.

Within a matter of days after Pearl Harbor,

This photo made in the early 1900's shows the White Pass yards, shops, and roundhouse at Skagway. (Provincial Archives of British Columbia)

Whitehorse, (Yukon River in foreground) terminus of the White Pass, looked like this in the early 1900's. (Provincial Archives of British Columbia)

the ground work was started for building the Alaska Highway. In the spring of 1942, a major point for construction was Whitehorse, a point deep in the heart of the Yukon supplied by the White Pass Railway. Supplies could be barged safely into Skagway, up the protected inland waterway.

Once again, the White Pass played a major role in a human drama deep in the far-northland. Just then the White Pass was not equal to the challenge. The narrow gauge was a financially starved and run-down railway. It owned less than a dozen working steam engines. Only two of these were new; the others were all more than thirty years of age. The roadbed was in poor shape. After all, the White Pass was geared for a modest amount of traffic. The railroad was low in everything except morale.

When the flood of traffic descended, there was trouble. Yet, somehow the railroad man-

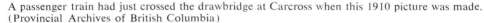

A passenger train had just crossed the drawbridge at Carcross when this 1910 picture was made. (Provincial Archives of British Columbia)

Pioneer and modern railroaders have battled the snows of White Pass. Above, a diesel rolls up to a section house at Summit; in the background is the U. S.-Canada snowshed. Below, this was a scene in 1910 on Tunnel Mountain. (Both Photos: Dedman's Photo Shop)

SNOW!

~~~~~~

Above, a caterpillar bulldozer, typical of modern equipment used to clear tracks, parks to await a train at point about 18 miles from Skagway. Below center: railroaders pose by a rotary snowplow at Clifton in the early 1900's. Below right: a rotary snowplow operates against the backdrop of the Sawtooth Mountains, 17 miles from Skagway. (All Photos: Dedman's Photo Shop)

aged to move 67,496 tons of freight in nine months. Because of the railroad's vital role in defense, the United States Army stepped in and assumed responsibility for operating the railway. Although a Canadian law prohibited foreign corporations from doing business in Canada, the Canadian government took legal action for the exception. The Canadians willingness for the American entry was understandable, for the Japanese had landed in force on the Aleutian Islands.

The United States government leased the White Pass for the duration, effective at 12:01 a.m. October 1, 1942. The 770th Railway Operating Battalion of the Military Railway Service took over all train operations, but kept the White Pass's own civilian veterans.

Motive power was needed and engines were immediately sent north from the "South 48." A pair of 10-wheelers (No.10 and No. 14) came from the East Tennessee and Western North Carolina; a pair of 2-8-0's (No. 20 and No. 21) arrived from the Colorado and Southern, and three 2-8-0's (No. 22, No.23, No. 24) came from the Silverton Northern. Seven Alco 2-8-2's (No. 250 and No. 256) arrived from the Rio Grande. In addition, one of the old defunct Klondike Mines Railway's little Baldwin locomotives, a 2-6-2 (the second No. 4) was bought and shipped from Dawson City to Skagway.

This strange and colorful assortment of narrow gauge locomotives was really not too unusual for the White Pass. After all, the railroad at one time or the other ran a three-track Climax, a pair of Vauclain compounds, 4-4-0's, Moguls, and 10-wheelers. Their newest engines were Baldwin Mikes built a few years earlier.

In 1943, the United States government sent ten 2-8-2's of War Department design north to Skagway. These originally were intended for Iran, but the military there optioned for diesels. They were constructed as meter gauge, so

Smoke billows from a rotary snowplow which otherwise would be virtually hidden in snow near White Pass summit at the peak of Winter. (Dedman's Photo Shop)

A fleet of rotary snowplows crosses a bridge enroute to keep the narrow gauge tracks open for vital traffic. (Dedman's Photo Shop)

they were quickly converted and modified for the thirty-six inch track.

With this assortment of power, the Army and the White Pass moved mountains of freight. Hundreds of thousands of tons of military machinery and equipment poured north and over the White Pass. The sleepy town of White-horse became a military camp.

Construction of the Alaska Highway started in March, 1942. The 1,500-mile highway from Dawson Creek, British Columbia, to Fairbanks, Alaska, was completed in nine months. The immense work load placed on the railway was great beyond belief.

The joint engine and freight car roster of the White Pass and the United States Army was something like this:

White Pass, 10 engines;
M.R.S., 26 engines.
White Pass, 38 freight cars
M.R.S., 253 freight cars.

In the last three months of 1942, the railway moved 25,756 tons of material. In 1943 (after the arrival of the ten W.D. 2-8-2's) the White Pass moved 281,962 tons over the 110-mile narrow gauge line. This equaled ten years of pre-war freight business!

Steam reigned in the mid-1950's when Locomotive 73 rolled onto the Skagway docks to meet the freighter Clifford J. Rogers, built for the White Pass system as a link with Vancouver, B. C. (Dedman's Photo Shop)

During World War II, the company's sternwheelers did a yeoman's service. The vessels delivered material to remote Alaska Highway construction sites situated near the Yukon's inland lakes and waterways. The river steamers operated until late fall — far beyond their normal season — because of the urgency of the Alaska Highway and the immense quantities of material required to build it. Despite ice and low water, the huge loads arrived on time without loss of freight and without serious damage to the faithful steamboats.

The war years brought hell to the White Pass. Gales, snow drifts, and frequent thirty below temperatures came during February, 1943, and January 1944, but neither the Army nor the White Pass civilians gave up. The sixty-year-old Cooke rotary snow plows, aided by bulldozers and men with shovels, somehow kept the line open.

The white hell of snow plagued railway operations. Despite the efforts of the railroaders, the snow did close the line for ten days in 1943 and eighteen days in 1944. The railroad fought against odds. Engines froze to the rail and

drivers on government Mikes, too large in diameter, were slippery. The White Pass had trouble from the counterbalance weights of the outside-framed ex-Rio Grande engines, for these would hit ice ledges and lift the Mikes clear off the rails.

The winters of 1943 and 1944 were rough ones, but despite the rugged weather the White Pass moved the vital freight to the north. The war years were busy ones. For example, on August 4, 1943, thirty-eight trains ran north and south in just twenty-four hours, hauling a total of 3,446 gross tons of freight.

As did many soldiers, the narrow gauge fought World War II and the Yukon's worst winters in twenty-five years. The line worked not with the best weapons possible, but with the equipment that was available. The line won and the freight was delivered.

For a salute to these years, War Department Locomotive No. 195 was chosen to be displayed permanently at the Trail of '98 Museum. She was moved to the site in 1962 to stand as a memorial to the war efforts of both the White Pass and the Military Railway Service.

60

THE GREAT BRIDGE

Snow covered the countryside when a White Pass and Yukon train crossed the steel bridge (top) over Dead Horse Gulch near the summit of White Pass soon after the structure's completion in 1901. Center, this photo taken during Fall, 1904, included the covered roundhouse and snow fence near the bridge. Below, a 1910 photo shows a train crossing the spectacular bridge. (All Photos: Provincial Archives of British Columbia)

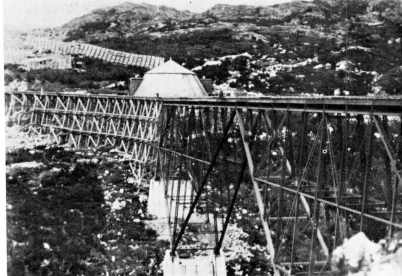

Locomotive 70, pulling 10 narrow gauge coaches, meets a ship at the dock in Skagway during the 1950's. (Dedman's Photo Shop, Skagway)

Locomotive 70, built for the White Pass in 1938, awaits passengers at the Skagway depot in 1945. The narrow gauge began to replace steam engines with diesels in the mid-1950's. The company retired this locomotive in 1963 and placed it in storage. (Dedman's Photo Shop)

Modern Narrow Gauge

CHAPTER IV

The White Pass and Yukon Corporation, Ltd., represents more than just a railway. A comprehensive and diversified transportation system, it begins on the wharves of Vancouver and terminates in the far northern reaches of the Yukon. In addition to its narrow gauge route, the White Pass provides motor ship, pipe line, and tractor-trailer truck services.

Following World War II, interest in northern Canada grew as the result of mining, oil exploration, prospecting, and efforts of the federal government of Canada. The volume of shipments, both in and out of the north, increased annually. An awareness of transportation costs and requirements accompanied this increase in volume.

Since the gold rush days, the White Pass moved mining machinery, gasoline, oil, food, and other necessities of life into the Yukon Territory. The line carried silver, lead, zinc, cadmium, copper, asbestos, and other material to the south.

While the White Pass and Yukon began as a narrow gauge, its expansion into ships, motor trucks, and pipe lines has made it able to serve its territory in many ways.

Despite diversification and the fact that the White Pass Railway is the shortest in actual route miles of all operations, the narrow gauge is the largest in value. The railway also is indispensable for service to the area.

There is no highway linking the Pacific Ocean and the Yukon River at Whitehorse. A tedious road goes from Haines to Haines Junction and then back to Whitehorse. A proposed road from Skagway due north through the mountains into Whitehorse probably is years away. The rugged terrain and cruel climate will make it difficult to complete such an all-weather route for cars and trucks.

Just as in the gold rush days, only a narrow gauge railway can compete with nature in the raw.

Most of the odd assortment of locomotives went south with the army following World War II. Only a 2-8-0 (No. 23) from the Silverton Northern, the 2-6-2 (second No. 4) from the Klondike Mines, and the government Mikes (No. 190 and No. 200) remained behind.

The pioneer White Pass Baldwins (No. 70 and No. 71) were ready for retirement. The post-war White Pass had little room for "tea kettles" or tired, patched old locomotives. The railway needed healthy power. In 1947, the company purchased two more 70-series Baldwin 2-8-2's (No. 72 and No. 73). After their arrival, the six 2-8-2's (No. 70, No. 71, No. 73, No. 80, and No. 81) handled most of the traffic. While occasionally they were assisted by the government 2-8-2's, the six locomotives usually could handle all the traffic.

While the White Pass was willing to continue operations with oil-burning steam engines, the line was unable to do so. The railway needed more power, but engine builders were constructing diesel units exclusively. Steam service was doomed.

Eyeing the changing technology, the White Pass management decided to acquire a narrow gauge diesel to be built to the line's specifications. It would require custom tailoring to meet specialized situations. The engines needed to absorb a high buff stress from snow slides. The diesel locomotive would operate all the way from sea level to more than 2,900 feet as well as in sixty-five degree below zero weather in gale force winds. That wasn't all. They could not have more than 27,000 pounds of weight per driving axle (E-27 Cooper's bridge rating) and they must negotiate a twenty-four degree curve.

Moreover, the White Pass insisted on a one-year trial period before final acceptance of the units.

The Erie Works of General Electric was selected to build the diesel locomotives to the narrow gauge's exacting specifications.

The first of the General Electric units (No.

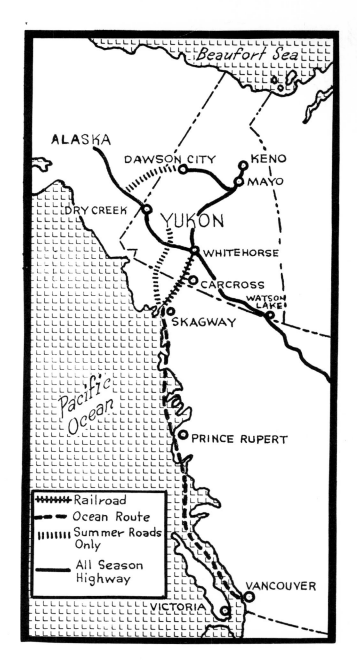

90 and No. 91) arrived in 1954. They were six motor box cab C-C units with six cylinder 800 horse power diesel engines. Each weighed 162,000 pounds and provided 24,000 pounds tractive effort. They were a huge success with their reinforced sloping noses and rail flangers instead of pilots. A pair of the diesel units could pull 410 tons from Skagway over the White Pass to Whitehorse without a helper. The White Pass paid about $160,000 each for its

A W. P. & Y. train rolls past Lake Bennett in the late 1960's. The area's growth increased freight and passenger traffic. (Dedman's Photo Shop)

first five diesel engines. The new locomotives not only reduced fuel expenses sixty percent, but also behaved well in the snow.

The first five units proved adequate for normal operations, and shoved steam into standby status. In 1963, the four 70-series Mikes served occasionally for extra passenger movements, yard assignments, and the rotary fleets. They virtually vanished when General Electric delivered additional new 90's to boost the diesel fleet to eight units in April, 1963. The last of the steam locomotives (No. 72 and No. 73) were retired June 30, 1964.

This marked the end of the regular use of steam power on the White Pass.

The railway's ninth diesel locomotive went into service in 1967, and two more diesels were scheduled for service in 1969.

The diesel fuel, heating oils, and gasoline reach Skagway in tankers. The oil goes north in the four-inch line laid by the United States Army in 1942 and now a part of the White Pass system. The 106.5 mile pipeline lies on the White Pass right-of-way nearly all the way from Skagway to Whitehorse. The line has a capacity of 3,000 barrels per day, or two and one-half times Yukon's present petroleum consumption. The original design allowed for additional pumping stations, and, if installed, would raise the capacity to 6,000 barrels per

The White Pass vessel Clifford J. Rogers was designed to carry freight in containers to be transferred to rail cars in Skagway.

day, or five times Yukon's present requirements.

Gasoline and similar fuels go by rail in a fleet of tank cars. The typical tank has a capacity of 6,500 gallons and is mounted on a flat car. The White Pass seeks to have six to twelve cars going, a similar number returning, and six to twelve cars being filled.

Assorted dry freight has been a different story. The White Pass pioneered an efficient and economical container system for odd-lot freight.

Over the years hundreds of ships sailed the inside Passage and connected the outside ports with Skagway, Alaska. The first vessel built solely for the Yukon's ocean commerce was the White Pass and Yukon Route's four-thousand ton freighter *Clifford J. Rogers,* placed in service between Vancouver and Skagway in 1955. This ship played a most important role in the development and subsequent application of the little-known "container concept" of freight-handling, a technique since adopted by other freighting operations throughout the world.

Prior to the development of the "container system," freight between Vancouver and Skagway went by ships of other firms using conventional freight-handling methods. As was the custom in those days, freight was hoisted from the Vancouver docks and slung aboard the ship in large nets. Each package was handled a dozen or more times during its short journey from the supplier's warehouse to the ship's hold.

After arriving in Skagway, this procedure was reversed and the ship discharged its cargo onto the Skagway dock. Here the White Pass and Yukon Route received the freight, loaded it into the railroad's box cars, and hustled the cars off to Whitehorse. Endless sheets of paper designed to guide the goods through the stops and checks accompanied each package.

This wasn't good enough. While not booming, the Yukon and northern British Columbia were enjoying a period of healthy growth during the post-war period. Mining, prospecting, and exploration were on the upswing. Discussions centered around proposed hydro-electric developments and the possibilities of revitalizing the Yukon's once lucrative industry. These activities by the early 1950's were producing slight increases in the Yukon's freight traffic. With this growth came a growing awareness of transportation costs and their relationship to the Yukon's future.

The $1.6 million White Pass Motor Vessel *Clifford J. Rogers* was specially designed to carry two hundred and fifty "containers," plus a deck load of other freight. To accommodate her cargo, she was fitted with the heaviest handling gear on the West Coast of British Columbia and Alaska.

The first freight containers were 7'x8'x8' in dimensions. Each had a 400-cubic foot capacity. These all metal containers came in four types: heater, freezer, dry, and explosive. Each could hold approximately five tons of general freight. The heater and freezer containers could hold their loads at a pre-determined temperature ranging from plus fifty degrees to minus twenty.

Dry container pick-up and delivery permitted freight loading at the shipper's Vancouver warehouse. After loading, they were locked, sealed for Customs, and shipped without opening until they reached the Yukon consignees.

The high capacity freezer containers were loaded and shipped by White Pass packers at the company's Vancouver West Indie's dock. The present temperature was maintained by the freezer unit, an integral part of the container. Handling and breakage costs dropped to an all-time low. Business men liked the White Pass containers because goods arrived in showroom condition and time consuming damage claim applications were eliminated. Yukon homemakers liked them, too, because they brought fruit and vegetables to the family table as fresh as the day they were packed in Vancouver.

The *Clifford J. Rogers* plied between Vancouver, British Columbia, and Skagway, Alaska on a regular two week schedule throughout the year. Container loads of Yukon-bound freight were exchanged at the White Pass Skagway dock for a southbound containerized cargo of asbestos fiber from Cassiar, B. C., and unitized pallet loads of silver, lead, and zinc concentrates from the United Keno Hill Mines.

Constant research and experiment made the Ocean Division a lively member of the White Pass family of transportation services and a respected partner of the historic White Pass

Riding the W. P. & Y. in the last half of the 20th century promises to offer spectacular scenery just as it did in the gold rush era. This train is on Tunnel Mountain. (Dedman's Photo Shop)

67

The White Pass motor vessel Frank H. Brown began linking Vancouver and Skagway in 1967, carrying containers that can be transferred to rail cars.

Railway. The *Rogers* in ten years made 247 round trips between Skagway and Vancouver.

In 1963, with the purchase of the three new diesel units, the White Pass started planning an improved container route with greater carrying capacity and increased freight handling efficiency. Plans called for an $8 million ship, new docks, modern terminals, and the most modern automated freight handling equipment available. Two years later the advanced design container ship *Frank H. Brown* made her maiden voyage.

This new White Pass ship was not designed for beauty, but for her versatility and efficiency. Costing more than $5 million, the 6,000 deadweight ton *Frank H. Brown* was launched April 22, 1965, at Canadian Vickers Shipyard Ltd. in Montreal. She was constructed from plans prepared by Gilmore, German, and Milne, naval architects.

The new container ship was named after Frank H. Brown, president of the White Pass and Yukon Corporation Ltd., who from 1954 to 1955 directed the original development of the "Container Route" and the construction of the original ship, the *Clifford J. Rogers*.

The new ship, 394 feet long, 70 feet wide, and with a speed of 13½ knots, completed sea trials and arrived in Vancouver on October 17, 1965, after a twenty-eight day voyage through the Panama Canal. Following more trials in local waters, the ship, spic and span and loaded with new containers, made her first run to Skagway. The *Rogers* made her last scheduled voyage on November 25, and was retired.

When the firm began expanding and diversifying, it reorganized and changed its name. The White Pass and Yukon Railway Co., Ltd., became the White Pass and Yukon Corporation Ltd. The new company acquired the British Yukon Railway Co., the British Columbia Yukon Co., the British Yukon Navigation Co., Ltd., and the Pacific and Arctic Railway and Navigation Co. In 1962, the company acquired the Loiselle Transport, Ltd.

The main office of the White Pass is in Vancouver, British Columbia. Officers in the late 1960's included F. H. Brown, president; N. F. W. H. D'Arcy, vice president; A. P. Friesen, vice president, managing director, and secretary, and F. D. Smith, treasurer. Directors were C. J. Rogers, R. D. Baker, R. C. Heim, H. L. Faulkner, Sidney Hogg, William Manson, M. H. Crichton, G. F. MacDonnell, Brown, and D'Arcy. The company had approximately 1,400 stockholders and in all operations employed nearly 600 people.

Frank H. Brown, president of the Vancouver-based White Pass system, directed development of the container plan.

Despite the company's entry into more diversified means of transportation, the railway portion of operations promised to remain important even in the 1970's. Annual reports showed that the rail properties accounted for approximately two-thirds of the company's $18 million in assets.

The White Pass system's diversification and efficiency in recent years enabled the company to resume dividend payments after its many lean years. Per share dividends have ranged from 20 to 40 cents annually in recent years. The shares are traded on the Vancouver, Toronto, and London stock exchanges.

David P. Morgan labeled the White Pass "America's Only Modern Narrow Gauge" in an article in the March, 1963, issue of *Trains Magazine* and other railway experts also praise the system.

The comprehensive ship-train-truck transportation system of today is a far cry from the narrow gauge railroad envisaged by its builders — Heney, Hawkins, Hislop, and Graves in

A. P. Friesen, vice president and managing director of the White Pass and Yukon Corporation, Ltd., helped direct the firm's expansion. Below, the motor vessel Brown docks at Skagway.

A cargo goes from a White Pass vessel to rail cars for transportation inland. Below left, this giant "straddle" carrier makes the transfer easy. Below right, this container carries lead and zinc concentrates by rail car from a mine in the Yukon Territory.

70

1898. They saw a continuing expansion of Yukon's mining industry centered on the Klondike goldfields, with other rich developments eventually adding their wealth to a burgeoning North.

Robert W. Service, caught up in the mood of the times, wrote: "Bob Smart's Dream," which told of stamping mills and smelters filling the air of Whitehorse with the sulphurous smoke of industry and the din of commercial activity. But the gold seekers and the dreamers departed, leaving the Yukon much the same as they found it.

To ensure that the rail line could handle future Yukon tonnage, the White Pass started a complete railway modernization program in 1953. This included large investments in heavier rail, and new repair shops.

Thousands of tourists annually travel over the White Pass in the narrow gauge's comfortable parlor cars during the beautiful warm Yukon summers.

The narrow gauge boasts proudly that parlor cars compose two thirds of its passenger equipment. The White Pass owns two coaches, two baggage cars, two combines — and twenty-one parlor cars.

When summer comes, there's not a seat too many.

The railroad's rolling stock also included approximately one hundred and ninety flat cars, thirty-six tank cars, two depressed center flat cars, two Cooke rotary snow plows, and a gasoline shop switcher.

Tourism to the area is becoming more popular. Among the vessels putting into Skagway with visitors during the summer are Canadian National's *Prince George*, Canadian Pacific's *Princess Louise*, and Alaska Cruise Lines' *Glacier Queen* and *Yukon Star*.

The picturesque narrow gauge attracts many rail fans, and the railway obligingly caters to visitors by providing them with unforgettable trips. The *Carcross Tour Special* ticket offers tourists a one-day, all-expense trip. The Skagway-Carcross round-trip* (departure at 8:30 a.m. and return at 4:05 p.m.) includes a parlor car seat and lunch. Passengers thrill at the

Locomotive 98, a diesel that replaced steam power in the mid-1950's, awaits service in the railway yards in 1966. (Dedman's Photo Shop)

twenty-one mile ascent to White Pass from tidewater and enjoy the twenty-six mile ride along Lake Bennett. On a "Carcross Turn," a pair of General Electric diesels can handle eleven parlor cars and more than 342 people! Largely because of these *Specials*, the railway counts on passengers for eight per cent of its total rail revenues.

Thousands of travelers describe this spectacular Trail of '98 rail tour as the highlight of their northern adventure.

Mountains, glaciers, and deep canyons unfold as the White Pass train climbs — three thousand feet in twenty miles — to historic White Pass summit. The original Trail of 1898 is clearly visible from the coach. The pioneer trail from Skagway to the Klondike is right beside the track.

At Lake Bennett, where sourdoughs built their boats, a complimentary "all you can eat" lunch is served in good old Yukon style. Good food and hearty appetites have made this meal famous throughout the north.

Leaving Bennett, the train follows the shores of the lake, famous for its magnificent setting

and beautiful reflections. It arrives at Carcross, Yukon Territory. Once an important Gold Trail town, Carcross is now the spa of the north. Hundreds of summer cottages dot the lake shore and countryside. Here, too, are the old stern-wheeler steamboat, *Tutshi*, the famous little locomotive, *The Duchess*, the old Caribou Hotel and Mathew Watson's General Store. A visit to Carcross is truly a peek into history.

After leaving White Pass Summit on the return journey, the train makes a "camera stop" at Inspiration Point, where passengers can "shoot" some of the most magnificent scenery in North America.

You can ride all the way, of course, on the five days-a-week mixed trains — No. 1 and No. 2 — even in the winter. Then you can try the "Family Package Plan" between Whitehorse and Skagway as we did in June, 1965. Automobile and two passengers were carried for $65, with the "all you can eat" lunch at Bennett's thrown in. The one-way fare at the time was $19.00. Ours was a more eventful trip than usual.

We loaded our car on a flat Friday in Whitehorse, and climbed aboard southbound No. 2 for Skagway. Thursday, the day before, four crew members were injured when two GE diesel units (No. 93 and No. 95) and nine cars of ore concentrate in containers went over a steep embankment about eight miles north of Skagway.

Water from a small creek weakened an earthen fill so it collapsed when the lead unit of the southbound train hit the embankment. Although the diesel units plunged down the bank along with the cars of ore concentrate, no passengers or open platform parlor cars were involved. The automatic braking system saved the rear end of the train.

The engineer was injured, along with the fireman and a dispatcher who was riding in the lead unit. The second unit rolled over and over with the head-end brakeman hanging on for

Northbound and southbound mixed passenger-container trains meet during the late 1960's at Lake Bennett, where the sour-doughs of 1898 built rafts and boats to float down the Yukon River to the Klondike gold fields.

Passengers relax on the observation coach of the "Carcross Turn" train. This picture was made in the mid-1960's. (Alaska Travel Bureau)

The author took this photo of the wreck that occurred when he was riding the narrow gauge in 1965. Debris of nine ore cars is in foreground.

the 700 feet to the bottom of the canyon. He escaped with minor injuries. Both diesels were severely damaged, and the steep canyon walls prevented an immediate salvage attempt.

Regular service resumed the next day, with passengers walking along a trail over and around the break. The bridge gang and work crews labored around the clock building a trestle to span the slide area. Freight was sidetracked at Clifton and White Pass siding during the construction.

By Saturday evening, slightly more than forty-eight hours after the derailment, the first of the sidetracked freight and our car moved downgrade to Skagway. The two diesel units were salvaged in the summer of 1966, even though the head unit went 200 feet and the second unit rolled 700 feet down to the canyon bottom.

Such accidents are uncommon on the White Pass. But when they happen, the workingest narrow gauge in the United States continues with business as usual.

In 1898 thousands of sourdoughs struggled inland from Skagway, across the magnificient St. Elias Mountains to Lake Bennett. There they cut timber and built boats and rafts to sail to Dawson and the rich gold creeks of the Klondike.

The old trail is still there. So is the Old Bennett Church, the White Pass, and Dead Horse Gulch. The White Pass and Yukon Railway follows the Trail of '98, which made the name Klondike ring around the world, and the yesterdays are there for all to see — right beside the railway track.

Today, a far cry from its start at the turn of the century, the White Pass is carrying tourists and freight in ever-increasing numbers and amounts. The narrow gauge of the north is the key to the growth of the Yukon.

It's a safe bet Sir Thomas, Mike Heney, and Sam Graves would approve of the railway's progress and development.

WHITE PASS & YUKON ROUTE

This monument to the pack animals of 1898 stands at Inspiration Point on the narrow gauge; Dead Horse Gulch is below. (Dedman's Photo Shop) Below, the White Pass Railroad building, erected in 1900, became a Skagway landmark. (Cy Martin Photo) OPPOSITE PAGE: Top, mountains rise spectacularly near Skagway in this photo made in the 1960's. Below, this 1969 picture shows the Arctic Brotherhood Hall, built in 1899, and the Golden North Hotel. (Both Photos: Dedman's Photo Shop)

Above, the pioneer locomotive "Duchess" is displayed at Carcross. Left center, a White Pass train rolls into Carcross in July, 1966. Lower left, this plaque at Carcross notes the railroad's completion. (Cy Martin Photos) Below, railroad passengers can see the Carcross dock, including a retired gold rush riverboat. (Alaska Travel Bureau)

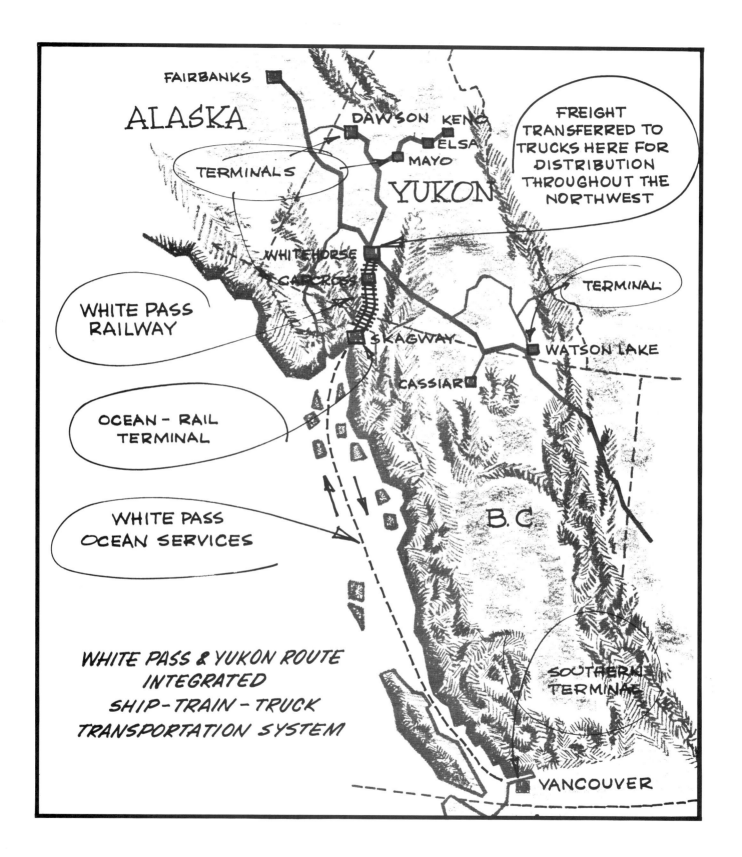

FAIRBANKS

ALASKA

DAWSON KENO

ELSA

MAYO

YUKON

TERMINALS

FREIGHT TRANSFERRED TO TRUCKS HERE FOR DISTRIBUTION THROUGHOUT THE NORTHWEST

WHITEHORSE

CARCROSS

TERMINAL

WHITE PASS RAILWAY

SKAGWAY

WATSON LAKE

CASSIAR

OCEAN - RAIL TERMINAL

B.C.

WHITE PASS OCEAN SERVICES

WHITE PASS & YUKON ROUTE INTEGRATED SHIP - TRAIN - TRUCK TRANSPORTATION SYSTEM

SOUTHERN TERMINAL

VANCOUVER

THE WHITE PASS & YUKON RAILWAY

ON AUG. 17, 1896, GEORGE CARMACK AND TWO INDIAN COMPANIONS, SKOOKUM JIM AND DAWSON CHARLIE, DISCOVERED GOLD IN THE KLONDIKE VALLEY, AN EVENT WHICH TRIGGERED THE KLONDIKE GOLD RUSH OF 1897-'98. IT WAS EVIDENT FROM THE START THAT THE KLONDIKE COULD NOT BE SERVICED WITHOUT A PERMANENT TRANSPORTATION SYSTEM. BY CHANCE, BRITISH ENGINEER, SIR THOMAS TANCREDE, CLOSE BROS. REPRESENTATIVE SAMUEL H. GRAVES, AND CANADIAN RAILWAY CONTRACTOR, MICHAEL J. HENEY, MET AT SKAGWAY IN 1898. WITHIN HOURS "BIG MIKE" HENEY HAD AGREED TO BUILD A RAILROAD FROM SKAGWAY TO THE YUKON IF SIR THOMAS AND GRAVES WOULD PROVIDE THE FUNDS.
CONSTRUCTION BEGAN MAY 27, '98, AT SKAGWAY. BY JULY 21, A PASSENGER TRAIN WAS PLACED IN SERVICE AND IT OPERATED A DISTANCE OF FOUR MILES. THIS WAS THE FIRST TRAIN TO RUN IN ALASKA. BY FEBRUARY 18, 1899, THE TRACK CROSSED THE SUMMIT OF WHITE PASS AND BY JULY 6TH IT REACHED LAKE BENNETT, B.C.
RAILWAY CONSTRUCTION WAS COMPLETED JULY, 1900, AND THE FIRST THROUGH TRAIN FROM SKAGWAY ARRIVED IN WHITEHORSE AFTER WHITE PASS PRESIDENT, SAMUEL H. GRAVES, DROVE HOME THE "GOLDEN SPIKE" AT CARCROSS JULY 29, 1900.

Above, this log station serves the narrow gauge at Whitehorse, the line's terminus. Above right, this sign on the depot digests the railroad's history. (Cy Martin Photos) Below, here is the way Whitehorse looked in late 1969. (Dedman's Photo Shop)

THE OLD BENNETT CHURCH

THE OLD CHURCH WHICH STANDS ON THE HILL OVERLOOKING THE LAKE WAS BUILT IN 1899 UNDER THE AUSPICES OF THE PRESBYTERIAN CHURCH

OF CANADA. DR. J. ROBERTSON WAS THEN SUPERINTENDENT OF MISSIONS AND THE REV. J. A. SINCLAIR WAS THE MINISTER IN CHARGE.

AT THE TIME OF ITS CONSTRUCTION THERE WERE THOUSANDS OF GOLD SEEKERS ENCAMPED HERE BUILDING THEIR BOATS AND RAFTS FOR THE

LONG JOURNEY BY LAKE AND RIVER FROM BENNETT TO THE KLONDIKE. WITH THE SPRING THAW, THE ARMADA SET FORTH, LEAVING THE LITTLE CHURCH

WITHOUT A CONGREGATION.
THE LITTLE CHURCH HAS STOOD — SILENT AND EMPTY — EVER SINCE.

Above left, a sign by the tracks at Bennett's tells of the Presbyterian Church (above right) built in 1899 but left without a congregation over the years when goldseekers left. Below center, the narrow gauge passes ruins of the White Pass docks at Bennett's. (Cy Martin Photos) Bottom, a White Pass train pauses at Bennett Station, 40 miles from Skagway and 60 miles from Whitehorse. (Dedman's Photo Shop)

Above, here is the Cowley siding and railway maintenance station. Below, this scene shows the old customs house and snowshed at White Pass. Both pictures were made in Summer, 1965. (Cy Martin Photos)

Snow remains even during the Summer on this siding (above) just north of the Alaska-British Columbia boundary. Below, railroaders make-up a southbound train at Whitehorse. (Cy Martin Photos)

Above, passengers on the White Pass and Yukon Route take advantage of a stopover in Caribou Crossing to look at the picturesque riverboats which for years carried prospectors and sightseers bound for points along the Yukon River.

Below, the narrow gauge White Pass tracks appear so small here that they almost look as though they were intended for a miniature train instead of a working railroad hauling freight and passengers. The scene is at Lake Bennett.

This aerial photograph, made during the late 1960's, shows the busy W. P. & Y. route yards at Skagway, the line's southern terminus. (Dedman's Photo Shop)

This wooden trestle near Inspiration Point, just south of the summit of White Pass, was photographed by the author during a trip in the Summer of 1965.

This view (above) of the White Pass yards at Whitehorse was made in 1965. Below, the southbound excursion train meets the southbound mixed daily near Pennington, B. C., in Summer, 1966. (Cy Martin Photos)

Snow-covered mountains rise near the harbor at Skagway (above) as a passenger train meets a ship in the 1960's. Below, a train hauls lead-zinc ore from a mine in 1969. (Both Photos: Dedman's Photo Shop)

The White Pass motor vessel Frank H. Brown arrives in Vancouver, British Columbia, carrying freight containers transferred from narrow gauge cars in Skagway. (Jack Lindsay, Ltd. Photo-White Pass & Yukon)

Top left, there was virtually no snow on the Summer day in the late 1960's when this diesel drew tank and flat cars over bridge built in the early 20th century. Lower left, by contrast, Winter snows covered the area in this 1969 picture. Crews that built a new tunnel and site for new bridge replacing the old one in Summer, 1969, used buildings in foreground. (Both Photos: Dedman's Photo Shop) Above, narrow gauge rolling stock drawn by two steam locomotives heads over route in the late 1940's. (Canadian Pacific Photo)

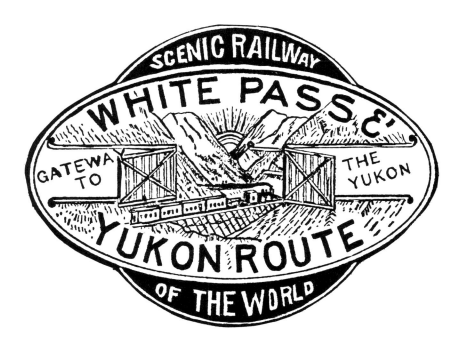

It gets a bit nippy up on the White Pass and Yukon Route. To make things comfortable, this railroader tends a stove in a passenger coach typical of the late 1960's. (Public Archives of Canada)

Roster of Equipment

STEAM LOCOMOTIVES

Name (or Number) and Date Acquired	Type	Builder	Date Built	Cylinders	Drivers	Weight (loaded)	Tractive Effort	Boiler Pressure	Bldr. No.
Duchess (1899)	O-(2)4-OT	Baldwin	1878	10x12	27¼	22,470	?	100 lbs.	4424
1 (1898)	2-6-0	Brooks	1881	14x18	42	95,500	12,975	135 lbs.	?
2 (1898)	2-6-0	Brooks	1881	14x18	42	95,500	12,975	135 lbs.	?
3 (1898) (1st #3)	2-8-0	Grant	1882	15½x20	36	98,600	16,000	140 lbs.	?
4 (1898) (1st #4)	4-4-0	Baldwin	1878	12x16	42	73,000	6,800	140 lbs.	4294
4 (1942) (2nd #4)	2-6-2	Baldwin	1912	15x20	37	120,000	16,000	160 lbs.	37564
5 (1898)	2-8-0	Baldwin	1885	15x18	36	100,000	15,100	150 lbs.	7595
6 (1899)	2-8-0	Baldwin	1899	19x11x20	38	159,000	21,000	200 lbs.	16455
7 (1899)	2-8-0	Baldwin	1899	19x11x20	28	159,000	21,000	200 lbs.	16456
8 (1900)		Climax	1897	14x14	30	100,000	?	150 lbs.	167
10 (1942)	4-6-0	Baldwin	1916	16x22	45	165,000	19,100	180 lbs.	42768
14 (1942)	4-6-0	Baldwin	1919	16x22	45	165,000	19,100	180 lbs.	52406
20 (1943)	2-8-0	Baldwin	1890	16x20	37	114,000	12,600	150 lbs.	11355
21 (1943)	2-8-0	Baldwin	1890	16x20	37	114,000	12,600	150 lbs.	11356
22 (1943)	2-8-0	Baldwin	1904	16x20	37	132,000	12,600	160 lbs.	24109
23 (1943)	2-8-0	Baldwin	1906	16x20	37	132,000	12,600	160 lbs.	27977
24 (1943)	2-8-0	Baldwin	1904	16x20	37	142,000	15,510	160 lbs.	24130
59 (1900)	4-6-0	Baldwin	1900	17x20	42	161,000	15,400	180 lbs.	17749
60 (1900)	4-6-0	Baldwin	1900	17x20	42	161,000	15,400	180 lbs.	17750
61 (1900)	2-8-0	Baldwin	1900	17x20	38	167,000	17,600	180 lbs.	17814
62 (1900)	4-6-0	Baldwin	1900	17x20	44	160,000	14,600	180 lbs.	17895
63 (1900)	2-6-0	Brooks	1881	14x18	42	82,100	10,600	135 lbs.	522
64 (1900)	2-6-0	Hinkley	1878	12x18	33	73,350	8,100	135 lbs.	?
65 (1900)	2-6-0	Brooks	1881-2	14x18	42	83,400	10,600	135 lbs.	?
66 (1901)	4-6-0	Baldwin	1901	17x20	42	161,000	15,400	180 lbs.	18964
67 (1901)	4-6-0	Baldwin	1901	17x20	42	161,000	15,400	180 lbs.	18965
68 (1917)	2-8-0	Baldwin	1907	19x20	42	214,000	24,000	180 lbs.	30998
69 (1908)	2-8-0	Baldwin	1908	21x22	42	214,000	24,000	180 lbs.	32962
70 (1938)	2-8-2	Baldwin	1938	17x22	44	238,000	21,600	215 lbs.	62234
71 (1939)	2-8-2	Baldwin	1939	17x22	44	238,000	21,600	215 lbs.	62257
72 (1947)	2-8-2	Baldwin	1947	17x22	44	238,000	21,600	215 lbs.	73351
73 (1947)	2-8-2	Baldwin	1947	17x22	44	238,000	21,600	215 lbs.	73352
80 (1940)	2-8-2	American Locomotive	1920	19x20	44	224,000	19,000	170 lbs.	61980
81 (1940)	2-8-2	American Locomotive	1920	19x20	44	224,000	19,000	170 lbs.	61981
190 through 200 (1943)	2-8-2	Baldwin	1943	17x24	48	211,000	16,000	185 lbs.	69425 through 69435
250 through 256 (1942)	2-8-2	American Locomotive	1923	18x22	44	354,500	22,790	200 lbs.	64981 64982 64983 64985 64986 64988 64990

GAS LOCOMOTIVE

3 (1942) (2nd #3)	0-4-0	Plymouth	1942	Gas Power	4471

DIESEL LOCOMOTIVES

90 through 92 (1954)	Diesel	General Electric	1954	See "Remarks"	32060 32061
93 and 94 (1956)	Diesel	General Electric	1956	See "Remarks"	32709 32710
95 through 100 (1963)	Diesel	General Electric	1963	See "Remarks"	32711 32592 34593 34594 35790 35791 35792
101 through 107 (1969)	Diesel	Alco (Montreal)	1969	See "Remarks"	602301 through 602307

Built in 1908 by Baldwin, Locomotive 69 served the White Pass until being retired in 1954. Two years later the 2-8-0 was sold to the Black Hills Central R. R. (Dedman's Photo Shop)

Notes

★

Duchess: Built as a 2'6" gauge 0-6-0T for Dunsmuir Diggle & Co.; sold to Wellington Colliery Ry.; sold to Atlin Southern Ry.; sold to White Pass in 1899 and widened to 3-foot gauge; first driver was not coupled when rebuilt, so engine was a 0-(2)4-0T. Retired 1919 and on display at Carcross.

No. 1: Believed to be an ex-Utah & Northern; ex-Columbia and Puget Sound (No. 3); sold to White Pass in 1898; rebuilt and renumbered 51 in 1900. Retired 1941 and on display at Whitehorse.

No. 2: Believed to be an ex-Utah & Northern; sold to White Pass in 1898; renumbered 52 in 1900; retired in 1940 and on display at Skagway.

No. 3 (1st No. 3): Built for the Cincinnati & St. Louis Ry. (No. 63); sold to Dayton & Ironton Ry. in 1884; sold to Columbia & Puget Sound Ry. (No. 9) in 1887; sold to White Pass in 1898; renumbered 53 in 1900 after being fitted with a new straight stack, extended smoke box, and new cylinders; scrapped in 1918.

No. 3 (2nd No. 3): Built 1942 as U.S.A. No. 7651; 175 h.p. gasoline-powered shops switcher; stilled used occasionally in 1960's.

No. 4 (1st No.4): Built for the Olympia & Tenino Ry., later called Olympia Chehalis Valley (No. 1); sold 1890 to Columbia & Puget Sound (No. 10); sold to White Pass in 1898; rebuilt and renumbered 54 in 1900; sold 1905 to Tenana Mines Ry. (No. 50); sold 1917 to Alaska Railroad; scrapped in 1930.

No. 4 (2nd No. 4): Built for Klondike Mines Railway (No. 4); sold to White Pass in 1944; sold in 1952 to Oak Creek Central Ry.; sold in 1965 to Petticoat Junction Railroad, Sevierville, Tenn.

No. 5: Built for Columbia & Puget Sound Ry. (No. 8); sold to White Pass in 1898; renumbered 55 in 1900; sold 1904 to Klondike Mines Ry. (No. 2); on display at Dawson City, Y. T.

No. 6: Built Jan., 1899, and first new locomotive purchased by White Pass & Yukon; renumbered 56 in 1900; rebuilt from Vauclain compound to simple in 1907; scrapped in 1938.

No. 7: Built Jan., 1899, for the White Pass; renumbered 57 in 1900; sold 1906 to Klondike Mines Ry. (No. 3); on display at Dawson City, Y. T.

No. 8: Built 1897 for Colorado & Northwestern Ry. (No. 2); sold to Pacific Contract Co. (No. 8); sold to White Pass in 1900; sold 1903 to Maytown Lumber Co.; scrapping date unknown.

Nos. 10 and 14: Both built for East Tennessee & Western North Carolina (Nos. 10 and 14); acquired 1914 by United States Army Transportation Corps (Nos. 10 and 14); both were damaged in a Whitehorse roundhouse fire in Dec. 1943; both were taken to Seattle and scrapped in Dec., 1945.

No. 20: Built Dec., 1890, for Denver, Leadville & Gunnison (No. 272); in 1899 became Colorado & Southern (No. 69); acquired by United States Army Transportation Corps. (No. 20) in 1943; scrapped Dec., 1945, at Seattle.

No. 21: Built Dec., 1890, for Denver, Leadville & Gunnison (No. 273); in 1899 became Colorado Southern (No. 70); acquired by United States Army Transportation Corps. (No. 21) in 1943; scrapped Dec., 1945, at Seattle.

No. 22: Built April, 1904, for Silverton Northern (No. 3); acquired United States Army Transportation Corps (No. 22) in 1943; retired in 1944; scrapped Dec., 1945, in Seattle.

No. 23: Built April, 1906, for Silverton Northern (No. 4) acquired by United States Army Transportation Corps (No. 23) in 1943; scrapped Dec., 1945, at Seattle.

No. 24: Built Dec., 1904, for Silverton, Gladstone, & Northerly (No. 34); sold 1915 to Silverton Northern (No. 34); acquired by United States Army Transportation Corps (No. 24) in 1943, retired 1944; scrapped 1951 at Skagway.

No. 59: Built May, 1900, for White Pass; scrapped in 1941.

No. 60: Built May, 1900, for White Pass; retired in Dec., 1942; placed as rip-rap in Skagway River at W. P. & Y. R. Milepost 2.5 in 1949.

No. 61: Built in June, 1900, for White Pass; retired in 1944; placed as rip-rap in Skagway River at W. P. & Y. R. Milepost 2.5 in 1949.

No. 62: Built in June, 1900, for White Pass; retired in 1945; placed as rip-rap in Skagway River at W. P. & Y. R. Milepost 2.5 in 1949.

No. 63: Built 1881 for Kansas Central Ry. (No. 102, renumbered No. 7); sold to White Pass in June, 1900; sold to Klondike Mines Railway (No. 1) in 1902; on display at Dawson City, Y. T.

No. 64: Built in 1878; early history unknown; Columbia & Western (Trail Tramway) (No. 2); Canadian Pacific Railroad (No. ?); Acquired by White Pass in Spring, 1900; scrapped in 1918.

No. 65: Built in 1881 or 1882; believed to have been used by Utah & Northern; Columbia & Western (Trail Tramway) (No. 3); Canadian Pacific Railroad (No. ?); acquired by White Pass in Spring 1900; sold 1906 to Tenana Mine Ry. (No. 51); sold 1917 to Alaska Railroad; scrapping date unknown.

No. 66: Built May, 1901, for White Pass; retired 1953; cab used on No. 69.

No. 67: Built May, 1901, for White Pass; retired 1951; placed as rip-rap in Skagway River at W. P. & Y. R. Milepost ? in 1951.

No. 68: Built June, 1907, for White Pass; destroyed by rock slide at Milepost 15.6 on Aug. 17, 1917.

No. 69: Built June, 1908, for White Pass; retired 1954; sold in 1956 to Black Hills Central R. R. (No. 69 "Klondike Casey").

No. 70: Built May, 1938 for White Pass; retired in 1963 and stored.

No. 71: Built Jan., 1939, for White Pass; retired in 1963 and stored.

No. 72: Built in May, 1947, for White Pass; retired June 30, 1964, and stored.

No. 80: Built May, 1920, for Sumpter Valley Railroad (No. 20, renumbered No. 102); sold to White Pass in 1940; retired in 1958 and stored.

No. 81: Built May, 1920, for Sumpter Valley Railroad (No. 19, renumbered No. 101); sold to White Pass in 1940; retired in 1957 and stored.

Nos. 190 through 200: Built Feb., 1943, for United States Army Corps of Engineers as meter gauge for use in Iran; diverted to White Pass and converted to 3-foot gauge; disposed of as follows: *No. 190,* retired in 1946 and sold in 1960 to Tweetsie Railroad (No. 190, "Yukon Queen"); *No. 191,* scrapped in 1951; *No. 192,* retired in 1960 and sold in 1961 to Rebel Railroad (No. 192, "Klondike Kate"); *No. 193,* retired in 1946 and scrapped in 1951; *No. 194,* retired in 1946 and scrapped in 1951; *No. 195,* retired in 1946 and on display at Skagway; *No. 196,* retired in 1961 and stored; *No. 197,* retired in 1944 and scrapped in 1951; *No. 198,* retired in 1944 and scrapped in 1945 at Seattle; *No. 199,* retired in 1944 and scrapped in 1945 at Seattle; *No. 200,* retired in 1944 and scrapped in 1945 at Seattle.

Nos. 250 through 256: Built Sept., 1923, for Denver, Rio Grande, & Western (Nos. 470, 471, 472, 474, 475, 477, & 479); disposed of as follws: *No. 250,* scrapped at Seattle in 1944; *No. 251,* scrapped in Seattle in 1945; *No. 252,* scrapped at Ogden in 1945; *Nos. 253, 254, 255, & 256,* scrapped at Seattle in 1945.

Nos. 90 through 100: all identical and all built by General Electric for White Pass; weight, 162,000 pounds; maximum starting tractive effort at 25 per cent adhesion, 50,270 lbs.; continuous tractive effort at 10 mph, 25,000 lbs.; type C-C; 6 cylinder, 9x10.5; 800 h.p. with reinforced sloping noses, rail flangers, and bolt-on snow plows; equipped with dynamic braking.

Nos. 101 through 107: all identical and all built for White Pass by Alco (MLW — Montreal); delivered Summer, 1969; maximum starting tractive effort at 25 per cent adhesion, 53,590 lbs.; continuous tractive effort at 8½ mph, 40,000 lbs.

Bibliography

Berton, Pierre, *The Klondike Fever,* Alfred A. Knopf, New York, 1960.

Colorado Annual, 1966, Colorado Railroad Museum, Golden, 1966.

Container Route News, White Pass and Yukon Route, various issues.

Graves, Samuel H., *On The White Pass Payroll,* Chicago, 1908.

Hamilton, W. R., *The Yukon Story,* Mitchell Press, Vancouver, B. C., 1964.

Minter, Roy, "Historical Sketch of the Yukon Territory," *Western Miner,* Vol. 39, No. 8, August, 1966. Gordon Black Publications Ltd., Vancouver, Canada.

————, "Salt Water Sourdoughs," *North Magazine,* July/August, 1965.

————, "The Steel Went North," *North Magazine,* May/June, 1962.

————, White Pass and Yukon Route, Personal Communication.

Morgan, David P., "America's Only Modern Narrow Gauge," *Trains Magazine,* February and March, 1963.

Moody's Transportation Manual, Editions of 1963 & 1966.

Mulvihill, Carl E., White Pass and Yukon Route, Skagway, Personal communication.

Ogilvie, William, *Early Days on the Yukon,* Bell and Cockburn, New York, 1913.

Robertson, Frank G. and Beth Kay Harris, *Soapy Smith: King of the Frontier Con Men,* Hastings House, New York, 1961.

The Whitehorse Star, Whitehorse, Yukon Territory, various issues.

White Pass and Yukon Route, various advertising pamphlets.

★

Locomotive 71, a 2-8-2 built by Baldwin, is pictured at Skagway soon after being delivered in 1939. After being retired in 1963, the locomotive was placed in storage for possible future use. (Provincial Archives of British Columbia)

Index

NUMBERS IN PARENTHESES INDICATE ILLUSTRATIONS OR MAP REFERENCES

A mixed train rolls on the White Pass right-of-way clinging to a mountainside in this photo made in the late 1930's. The train was en route to Skagway. (Public Archives of Canada)